Hell in a Nutshell

Hell in a Nutshell

The Mystery of His Will

Charles Watson Sr.

RESOURCE *Publications* · Eugene, Oregon

HELL IN A NUTSHELL
The Mystery of His Will

Copyright © 2016 Charles Watson Sr. All rights reserved. Except for brief quotations in critical publications or reviews, no part of this book may be reproduced in any manner without prior written permission from the publisher. Write: Permissions, Wipf and Stock Publishers, 199 W. 8th Ave., Suite 3, Eugene, OR 97401.

Resource Publications
An Imprint of Wipf and Stock Publishers
199 W. 8th Ave., Suite 3
Eugene, OR 97401

www.wipfandstock.com

PAPERBACK ISBN: 978-1-4982-9003-6
HARDCOVER ISBN: 978-1-4982-9005-0
EBOOK ISBN: 978-1-4982-9005-0

Manufactured in the U.S.A.   09/22/16

This book is dedicated to my wife, Amy Watson, and our children, CJ, Jenna Marie, and Charity Faith. I long for the day when each of you comes to experience the extraordinary peace that accompanies an assurance in the doctrine of Universal Reconciliation. You are the most important people in this world to me. I love each of you deeply.

God's attributes should be the litmus test for sound theology; not the other way around.

Contents

Acknowledgments | ix
Abbreviations | x

Section 1: Preparation and Clarification | 1

Introduction: The Great Divide | 3
1   The Appetizer | 8
2   What's What? | 14

Section 2: Lifting the Veil | 21

3   Heretically Orthodox Faith | 23
4   Expiring Grace and Mercy | 31
5   Deficient Love | 40
6   Unscrupulous Justice | 47
7   Grace, Mercy, and Love vs Justice | 58

Section 3: The Mystery of His Will | 69

8   Biblically Unorthodox Faith | 73
9   Perpetual Grace and Mercy | 81
10   Relentless Love | 91
11   Victorious Justice | 99

12 Grace, Mercy, and Justice in Love: Holiness | 110

Epilogue: Urgency | 115

Appendix A: Questioning the Gospel | 125

Appendix B: Proof-texts | 129

Appendix C | 140

Appendix D: Book Recommendations | 141

Appendix E: George MacDonald on Adoption | 142

Acknowledgments

My mom, Cyndi Watson, who passed away far too early, albeit in God's timing. You are missed.

Amy Watson—a model wife and mother; a woman after God's own heart; the only woman for me; my good thing.

Justin Fowler—without your influence in my theological walk, I would never have embarked on this outstanding journey.

Clint Scott—you are a true friend. Iron sharpens iron, brother.

Robin Parry—*The Evangelical Universalist* has affected me deeply.

Gerry Beauchemin—*Hope Beyond Hell* was the first book that I read on the topic of Universal Reconciliation. The Lord is using you to affect many who need better news than is being presented by the church at large.

George MacDonald—your writings are theologically rich, but were overlooked for far too long. Your work will continue to change people's lives for years to come.

Thomas Talbott—*The Inescapable Love of God* moved me greatly. You are a man after God's own heart.

Wipf and Stock—thank you for seeing potential in my book and for giving me the chance to spread the really good news of Universal Reconciliation.

Our Good Good Father—thank you for not giving up on any of us!

Abbreviations

CD	Cognitive Dissonance
CI	Conditional Immortality (annihilation)
CU	Christian Universalism
ECT	Endless Conscious Torments
NT	New Testament
OT	Old Testament
UR	Universal Reconciliation

Section 1

Preparation and Clarification

BEFORE WE BEGIN, I would like to provide a brief overview of the structure of this book. This book consists of three sections. The first section includes the introduction and the first two chapters. The final two sections are of equal length and parallel each other in length and subject matter. Section 2 is preparatory for Section 3, just as the first section is an assemblage for that which follows. Section 1 consists mostly of background information about me—who I am and where I have been in my spiritual walk. The final two chapters of this section provide necessary information about what will be examined in the following sections.

Introduction

The Great Divide

> God, grant me the serenity to accept the things I cannot change, the courage to change the things I can, and the wisdom to know the difference.
>
> —REINHOLD NIEBUHR

As twenty-first-century Americans, Europeans, or whatever nationality with which we identify, few of us can imagine how our ancestors lived just a couple of centuries ago. Although the lifestyle of each new generation differs significantly from the previous one, we all share commonalities with those who lived before us. One such commonality is the human tendency to resist anything that challenges the way we view the world.

I have caught myself, on more than one occasion, resisting an idea simply because it was unfamiliar—because it caught me off-guard. Whenever this happens, I tend to go into fight or flight mode.[1] When I choose fight rather than flight, I usually become defensive because I, like everyone else, am committed to the way I see things. When I choose flight, I ignore the situation in hope that it will desist. Unfortunately, some itches just don't seem to go away.

Orthodoxy

The Merriam-Webster Dictionary defines "orthodox" as "conforming to established doctrine especially in religion." Within the Christian faith, we have established doctrines that vary from jots and tittles to much larger dissimilarities. Besides the minor differences that distinguish each

---

1. This is a physiological reaction that occurs in response to a perceived harmful event, attack, or threat to survival.

denomination from another, there are larger dissimilarities that differentiate entire systems of religion. Within the Christian religion, many seemingly do not understand the method by which our dissimilarities ought to be categorized; which has resulted in a tendency to condemn those who will not, or cannot, conform to "orthodoxy."

According to the Oxford English Dictionary, the origin of the English word "orthodox" comes from the Greek word *orthodoxos*. In order to obtain an accurate understanding of this concept, let's deconstruct the term. *Orthos* literally means "straight or right [correct]" and *doxa* means "opinion." Therefore, "orthodox" is literally rendered as the "correct opinion" of the masses.

Orthodoxy has been in a gradual state of (de)formation over the years, preferably toward objectivity as time marches onward. Much of what was considered "orthodox" during the first five centuries of church history is understandably quite different than what is accepted as orthodox today. Much is the same, but just as much is different.

At this point, you may be thinking, "Facts are just *that*—facts. They do not change. Truth is, and always will be, truth." It is common knowledge that the earth is, and always was, spherical, regardless of what was or is accepted by the most intelligent scientists and philosophers in the world. However, orthodoxy is not necessarily factual because it consists of truth *claims*. Truth claims are statements about what someone has come to believe about supposed existents. No "truth claim" is beyond a philosophical shadow of doubt. Otherwise, it would be a law, rather than a mere claim/proposition. Orthodoxy is only factual once it *aligns* with objectivity. Since a universal acceptance of any theological or philosophical idea does not determine its validity, how can we decide *when* orthodoxy has finally been perfected?

No one, at any point in history, arbitrarily determined the immutable details for Christian orthodoxy. How could they? The literal rendering of "orthodoxy" sheds some light on the historical development of what was, and has become, orthodox. At any given moment in church history, the prevalent understanding of theology has always been the "correct opinion" of the masses. Therefore, I suspect very few could dispute the fact that orthodoxy has been in, and remains in, a gradual state of change; although a few may endeavor.

Following the time when Jesus' original followers were given the derogatory title "Christian," there have been persistent and gradual modifications to what has been accepted as orthodox. From Jesus' victorious declaration- "It is finished!", up to and beyond the destruction of AD 70, throughout the Dark Ages, up to the pinnacle of the Great Awakening, and all the way to the present day, anyone who would daresay that orthodoxy has remained in its pristine first-century condition would destroy any credibility they may have had in the eyes of their peers.

As Christians, faith is the primary feature of our religion. It binds us together and sets us apart from every other religious system. Although the secular realm defines faith as belief in something for which there is little to no compelling evidence, Christians have obtained their definition of faith from what has determined every other aspect of our religion—the Bible: "Now faith is the substance of things hoped for, the evidence of things not seen."[2]

Apologists have often stated that biblical faith is by no means blind, but reasonable. If we, as Christians, are to uphold our biblical worldview, we *must* take our faith seriously. Even though countless Christians do just that, just as many professing believers fail to apply the scriptural teaching that their faith must be in Christ *alone*. Even though I believe Christianity is the one true religion, I refuse to pretend that everything about it is impeccable. Although the Bible's content is of God, corporate Christianity is not a theocracy.[3] Therefore, its practices and traditions are susceptible to misconceptions.[4]

The Bandwagon

The doctrine of hell has been a sensitive subject for as long as the concept has existed. Ever since the beginning of the Christian movement, the *Christian* doctrine of postmortem judgment has been prevalent, which had always consisted of *three* schools of thought. As is expected with opposing views, each school has been at odds from the onset. Since one camp has received more attention, as of late, than the others, I have come to realize that many, if not the majority, of churchgoers have not been taught that there is more than one Christian understanding of postmortem judgement.

For the sake of clarity, imagine someone who has never considered Christianity until fairly recently. Let's call this person Caleb. Caleb has never been anti-religious; he has simply never desired to pursue spirituality until recently. The only reason Caleb developed a newfound interest in Christianity was because his company asked him to relocate into a city that was in the center of the Bible Belt. After a month or so, something sparked deep within

---

2. Heb 11:1.

3. At least, not like that which Israel was under in the Old Testament.

4. Even before copies of the Bible were mass produced, the leaders of the Catholic Church were just as prone to misinterpretations as laymen.

the cavities of his soul as he observed his neighbors living their faith out loud. From the outside looking in, Caleb was able to learn quite a bit about the organized church. He was even able to connect the theological dots during sermons and classes provided at several local churches, in which he was beginning to develop several lasting friendships. His life was finally coming together.

Like many, Caleb had no idea that there was more than one Christian doctrine of postmortem judgement. For the longest time, he was oblivious to alternate points of view. One of the few pieces of information new converts have to consider when it comes to deciding what to believe about postmortem judgement is the prevalence of the doctrine in question. When I first came to Christ, I reasoned in a manner similar to Pascal's Wager, which suggests that it is safer to believe in God even if he does not exist because the consequences for disbelief are much higher if we are mistaken. I applied the same logic to hell—"It is safer to believe in Endless Conscious Torment (ECT) even if it is untrue, because the consequences for disbelief are much higher if I am mistaken.

Naturally, the eye is drawn toward the focal point of any given situation. Whether we are admiring a painting or pumping our fists in a football stadium, our eyes seem to know where to look. The same applies to religious beliefs. When there are several options available, that which has the most support from the populace naturally draws our focus and causes us to assume that there must be something "right" about it. Likewise, that which is rejected by the masses usually leaves a suspicious pit in our stomachs.

Just as animals instinctively follow their flock, herd, etc., people intuitively follow the masses. If a group of people walks uniformly on any random side of an aisle, stragglers will be few and far between. I once saw a social experiment on the internet where a group of people stood with their backs facing the road at a bus stop. When others arrived, they did the same. There is something within our nature that drives us to blend in with our own kind. Subconsciously, we want to fit in; we want to be accepted. Consequently, we tend to resist diversity; especially when it comes to theology.

Since Christian Universalism is not presently accepted as an orthodox doctrine, many subconsciously assume that it has no credibility. When anyone challenges the prevalent doctrine of postmortem judgment, or any other prevalent doctrine, the typical reactions are somewhat conspicuous. Some reactions arise more frequently than others. Such as: "It's what the Bible teaches." "Scripture plainly says hell is forever." "You don't believe that God's Word means what it says."

One of my goals for this book is to address many of the points that are frequently argued back and forth on nearly every platform. It seems like every discussion on this subject has to work its way from the ground up, which is usually due to the lack of effort from at least one party.

I want this book to *serve* as a tool in the hands of anyone who desires to get past foundational conversations and further into sophisticated dialog. Even though this book is written primarily to those who believe in ECT, anyone can learn from it and enjoy the material. On the other hand, this book is also for the unbeliever whose disbelief hinges on the horrid doctrine of ECT. So this book is actually for anyone who condones ECT or rejects the Christian Faith while presuming the validity of this doctrine. It is for those who are committed to test *all things*,[5] just as it is for those who are willing to follow the truth, regardless of where it may lead.

---

5. 1 Thess 5:21a.

1

The Appetizer

THERE IS NOTHING PARTICULARLY impressive about me that qualifies my voice or pen to demand anyone's silence and undivided attention. No bells will ring at the mention of my name because it is of no merit to the general public. You have, in all likelihood, never heard of me or of any of my accomplishments. I am, by far, no C. S. Lewis or William Lane Craig. Neither am I officially qualified to speak authoritatively about theological or philosophical conundrums. As I admitted above, in relation to theological and philosophical academics, I am no one—probably much like you.

I have been blessed with an incredibly virtuous and beautiful wife who supports me as I pursue my dreams—even when we do not see eye to eye. Currently, we have three children: a son, CJ—the big brother of his two sisters—Jenna Marie and Charity Faith. For the first half of my Christian walk, which began in 1998, there was as much spiritual growth as you can expect from a child tip-toeing his way through his early adolescent years. Since I was not saved much earlier in life, the idea of ECT played a large part in my decision to pray the "sinner's prayer."[1] Although I was led to believe that salvation was kind of like fire insurance, there was much more depth to my faith than that. I genuinely believed in Jesus and accepted the plain essential truths of the Christian faith. Nevertheless, a sincere fear of being abandoned by God for all of eternity unmistakably nudged me along.

Since I was raised in a Southern Baptist. . . atmosphere, I took the concept of eternal security for granted. Jesus would never leave me nor forsake me[2]—of this I was sure.[3] Inevitably, doubt crept in. After many years of riding the seesaw of doubt and assurance, I succumbed to the pressure of my peers and explored the terrain of debauchery. I *knew* my fate was sealed,

---

1. "The sinner's prayer" is not a biblical concept.
2. Deut 31:6; Heb 13:5
3. Some agree that Jesus will never leave us nor forsake us, but reject the idea that we cannot leave or forsake him.

but subconsciously assumed it gave me the liberty to take advantage of my good fortune so that grace may abound. God forbid.[4]

According to the doctrine of eternal security, I could have chosen to sustain my Godless lifestyle. However, I was not afforded the luxury of doing so with a clear conscience as I would have prior to my encounter with Jesus. In hindsight, the doctrine of eternal security actually caused more day-to-day stress and anxiety than I could have predicted. I could not continue living according to my fleshly desires without *feeling* forsaken by Christ. I felt guilty for manipulating the system to appease my flesh, even though it was not usually intentional. I thirsted for the water I had been promised, yet failed to drink.

After several years of drugs, alcohol, and so on, my actions finally began to correspond with what is expected from a new creature in Christ.[5] As my old desires began to fade, new ones began to outweigh the old. By abandoning my worldly infatuations, I was then able to return to my first Love.[6] In the process, the friends I made when the sun went down became old friends as I surrounded myself with people who lived in the light. I became much more interested in philosophy, theology, and debate. Years later, I found myself passionate for the things of God. I explored several online debate groups, and founded another. I vigorously studied Scripture, philosophy, theology, and so on. Everything was just as I had always imagined it—that is, until I met Justin.

***

At this point, you have begun to form several judgments, which have likely birthed several interesting questions. You may have interpreted my youth as a detriment to whether or not I have enough life experience to have anything of value to contribute to what has been written elsewhere. Since many Christians, three to four times my spiritual age, are theologically and philosophically underdeveloped, that is understandable.

There would be little benefit to commenting either way about my spiritual development. Therefore, you will have to judge for yourself. I only ask that you read this book in its entirety before casting any significant judgments. When minor judgments surface, catch them before they develop into something that will interfere with how you interpret the material. Not

---

4. Rom 6:1.
5. Eph 4:24.
6. Rev 2:4.

unlike every other author, I have a specific message I want to convey. Therefore, your resolve is paramount to whether or not this book is successful.

As this book progresses, embrace questions as they arise and encourage their development. How else can iron sharpen iron as one person sharpens another?[7] Scripture commands us to *test* all things[8], to *judge* for ourselves what is right.[9] Ideas are tested most efficiently with sincere questions. But on the other hand, premature judgments are counterproductive. So please shy away from trying to answer your questions, or mine, prematurely. Also, even if you think you already know the answer to certain questions, try your best to remain neutral for the time being.

Because of my addictive personality, I am inclined to go overboard with anything that intrigues me. Close friends of mine would attest. From my rebirth up to this moment, I have been passionate about everything mentioned above. Therefore, one could imagine how much time I have invested in conversing with atheists and theists alike. For years on end, it was an important part of my life.

Around the beginning of January 2012, I had my first encounter with someone who was a professing Christian Universalist, which was a strange experience because, at the time, I believed that those two terms were mutually exclusive. As far as I was concerned, he was a heretic. Although I had dealt with my fair share of "wolves in sheep's clothing", I was unprepared for what followed.

Whenever a Christian rebukes another professing believer, they believe that their accusations are justified. Otherwise, they would not bother doing so. Those who organized the inquisitions and witch hunts certainly felt more than justified to do what they saw as the Lord's work. Who could have been more sincere than those who shouted, "Crucify him!" at the foot of the cross? History has proven that Christians have been no less guilty of falsely labeling people as heretics as the penal system has been of sending innocent civilians to death row.

As I reminisce on the beginning stages of what resulted in my paradigm shift, I regret how I condemned Justin as a heretic before I understood his position. In grace, he did not retreat, but boldly, yet gently, presented the doctrine of Universal Reconciliation (UR); which I interpreted as a test from God. This heretic was walking on holy ground and he did not remove his shoes. He was pushing a false teaching that negated any need for the cross. As a brother in Christ, he needed correction before he slid out of control on

7. Prov 27:17.
8. 1 Thess 5:21.
9. Luke 12:57.

the slippery slope of bad faith. God forbid he became apostate—that is, if he was even a "true Christian" to begin with.[10]

According to Dr. Wayne Dyer, "The highest form of ignorance is when you reject something you don't know anything about." Although the church has dutifully and necessarily anathematized many who were actual heretics,[11] many innocent Christians have been condemned with the lot. Those who fail to learn from history are doomed to repeat it. We must be careful not to repeat past mistakes.[12] Granted, those who participated in the inquisition may have had a genuine desire to remain loyal to God, to defend his name, and to protect the brethren from heresy, but authenticity does not justify savagery. I believe that the general feeling of fear that comes along with the traditional understanding of postmortem judgment is ultimately to blame. "What people revere, they resemble, either for ruin or for restoration."[13]

Investigating the Enemy

The enemy had crossed the border of orthodox Christianity with no arsenal beyond what was, from my point of view, wishful thinking. My crosshairs were set. I did not know much about Justin, but I was convinced that this was a problem that demanded my undivided attention. A simple ban would not suffice. A "ban hammer" was adequate when dealing with militant anti-theists on online forums, but Justin was a special case. He *seemed* to carry the Christian banner, but rejected what I believed was a pillar to the Faith. I could not fathom how a Christian could believe something that conflicted with the "plain" reading of the Bible.

For instance, take Matthew 22:14: "Many are called, but few are chosen." How could anyone misinterpret the plain reading of this verse? What could it mean besides that many who think they are saved will be eternally separated from God, that only a few will be saved? What about the passage which states that those whose names are not found written in the Lamb's Book of Life will be cast into the lake of fire? I was dumbfounded when I learned that his paradigm taught that even the devil and the fallen angels

10. I have a blog post on this subject at www.CharlesWatsonSr.com.

11. For example, Gnosticism, Arianism, Docetism, and Nestorianism.

12. Origen's universalism is a perfect example. He was not anathematized until hundreds of years after his death—long after he was around to defend himself. His belief in the preexistence of the soul was rightly deemed heretical. Many have deemed his universalism as guilty by association.

13. Beale, G. K. We Become What We Worship. Downers Grove, Ill.: IVP Academic, 2008. Print.

would be restored. (Later, I found out that this is a matter of contention among those who believe in Universal Reconciliation.) I could have swept everything under the rug by banning him before he could do any more damage, but that would have made the administration team appear weak and hypocritical. We had always purported that our faith was not blind, but reasonable. God had provided a perfect opportunity to practice what we preached.

Several hours after Justin presented his case for CU, I posted a thorough critique of his presentation. To my surprise, he was delighted with my timely response and promised to reply promptly. I anticipated that he would return humbled and repentant. How could I possibly have failed when God was so clearly on my side, right? The following day, Justin returned as promised. Did he have a change of heart overnight? Did I play a role in turning him into a new man? To my surprise—which happens much more often than I expect—nothing turned out as I had anticipated. Although his response was written with gentleness and respect, it was nearly impossible to read those qualities into that which challenged what I considered essential to the Faith.

Only after dissecting his presentation did I catch a whiff of something that was totally alien, yet bittersweet. I had only just realized the difference between Christian Universalism and Unitarian Universalism (UU); first of which claimed to be evangelical, not only in what it affirmed, but also in what it denounced. I had barely scratched the surface of just a few points of Justin's theology. Even though it was intriguing, my point of view remained the same. Once I looked into it a bit further, I came to realize that my mission to debunk this heresy had only just begun. I spent the next six months studying and arguing against Christian Universalism from every possible angle. I read books in favor of Justin's view just as I read books that argued against it.

Each day, within this six month period, was just as intense as the first. The most difficult aspect of it all was how I did not seem to make any progress until the final month or so. For the first four months, I faithfully[14] sought to disprove the doctrine rather than to test and consider its claims. I was loyal to the way I saw things. I had an unmovable faith in my theological convictions rather than in Him who is the Center of it—Jesus.[15]

On one rainy Saturday morning, it dawned on me. I realized that I had never tested my beliefs about hell. I had learned the art of apologetics quite well. I understood how to defend my beliefs, but had never tested them. I never realized that my beliefs were included in the "all things" that scripture

---

14. That is, faithful to my presuppositions.
15. This is not to say that I did not have faith in Jesus.

tells us to test. This breakthrough enabled me to make some actual progress in this journey on which I had embarked. The first technique I used to test my presuppositions was called "playing devil's advocate," which allowed me to see my beliefs from a perspective outside of my own. You would be surprised at how differently things looked from the outside looking in.

I always understood the doctrine of ECT as the default interpretation of postmortem judgment, as something that is essential to the Christian Faith. I considered any other theory or opinion on this subject as either heretical or, at best, liberal. Soon thereafter, I came to to realize that I did not know as much as I thought. How many of us do? I came to acknowledge that I habitually labeled those who disagreed with me about any given doctrine either as deceived or mistaken. I assumed that everyone would eventually come around to see things the right way—my way. At the time, I did not understand something that all Christians must understand in order to be effective as evangelicals- the difference between essential and nonessential doctrines. Like many, I treated everything I believed as though it was essential to my faith. Our convictions are so interwoven that it is easy to become so frustrated with its tangles and knots that we give up and accept that everything is "just the way it is."

I would describe this six month period as one of the most spiritually intense seasons of my life. I could never thank Justin enough for introducing me to something that makes perfect sense of my life, something that patches all the tears and holes Calvinism and Arminianism have ripped and burned into the Christian fabric for centuries. Thanks to this doctrine, I can now worship God with a greater joy than I could have ever imagined. I now see the glorious truths of UR in music, sermons, and Sunday school lessons, just to name a few—most which are unintentional by the teacher, pastor, or musician.

Even though I thought I knew what Christ meant when he spoke of a peace that surpasses all understanding, it was not until I came to accept the truth of Universal Reconciliation that I began to experience something I can only describe as *all-peace*. It seems impossible to explain spiritual actualities in a physical domain adequately. I pray that as you read this book, you do so with a heart softened enough for the Holy Spirit to move freely within you. There will be a sense of hesitancy since we all resist change, but that feeling will pass once you begin seeing Scripture fit together with far fewer seams than ever before.

2

What's What?

WHEN I WAS ORIGINALLY introduced to CU, my theological development was anything but primitive because I had invested a lot of time into studying the mainstream understanding of biblical concepts. I even had a moderate amount of interest in understanding doctrines that were rejected as unorthodox, if only to become more proficient at defending orthodoxy. Regardless of how much effort I put into defending and promoting my passions, I eventually discovered that I had, somehow, never investigated Christian Universalism.

If you are unlike I was by being familiar with the ins and outs of each theological class of postmortem judgement—Endless Conscious Torments (ECT), Christian Universalism (CU), and annihilation/Conditional Immortality (CI)[1]—you may desire to skip this chapter altogether.[2] Some people prefer dessert (Section 3) prior to the main course, while others prefer to skip the appetizer (Section 1) so they will have more room for the main portion of the meal (Sections 2–3). Preferences are like appetites; we all have one that is unlike any other. As any culinary connoisseur would attest, the food that precedes the main course serves an important role. It serves its purpose—to whet the appetite, to herald what is to come.

Do not be discouraged by a lack of depth just yet. Excavators understand that they must first map out the lithosphere before they can successfully mine for gold or diamonds in the rough. You can pick up a shovel and dig randomly in your yard if you wish, but your chances of striking it rich are minimal without sufficient planning and preparation. Therefore, before we jump headlong into searching for hidden treasures, we must first brush away the dust so we can see what we are working with.

---

1. CI and Annihilation are not exactly the same, but they do share numerous commonalities.

2. Chapter 3 begins the main course of this book.

Endless Conscious Torments

In America, and likely anywhere else the Christian faith prevails, the doctrine of ECT is drilled into our minds as soon as we are of age. The grisliness of this doctrine is, of course, veiled from little ears; but its basic ideas are taught to the youngest of our littlest ones to the most darlin' of our eldest faithful congregants. ECT basically claims that everyone who dies without washing their robes in the uncontaminated blood of Jesus[3] will stand before the judgment seat of Christ to give an account for everything they have done, whether good or bad.[4] Without Jesus as their Mediator, they will suffer forever for dying in their sins.

According to this doctrine, forgiveness and grace through Christ's atoning death, burial, and resurrection is only available before the death of our bodies. Those who die in their sins will have simply missed the boat. Once it catches wind, it is as gone as yesterday. Since grace is no longer available, so, too, is any chance for salvation. *It is appointed for man once to die, and after that comes judgment.*[5] Many will die while "knowing that they know that they know" that they are going to heaven when they die, but a portion of that many will be in for a rude awakening. Some will be apathetic. Others will cry out, "Lord, Lord," appealing to the fruit of their travail, but will be cast into the hell of fire along with the indifferent—in torment day and night, forever and ever[6]—perpetually conscious in a flame that never burns out nor diminishes in its intensity.

The following will continue endlessly throughout the ages: the flame, pain, agony, grief, sorrow, thirst, heartache, a sense of loss, regret, and cravings for all things desirable, including sleep, food, water, love, warmth, coolness, companionship, renewal, reconciliation, restoration, rest—relief. The intensity of each agony will never lessen. Jesus was born to save *many* from this fate. Those who reject Christ reject God and indirectly *choose* the postmortem horrors described above. God would not be impartial[7] if he saved anyone out of hell, if he snatched anyone out of the fire.[8] Whether we like it or not, this is what the Bible teaches. ECT is just because God is just, whether we understand it or not.

---

3. Rev 22:14.

4. 2 Cor 5:10. Although this passage applies primarily to Christians, everyone will have to stand before Christ.

5. Heb 9:27.

6. Rev 20:10.

7. Acts 10:34.

8. Jude 1:23.

When I refer to this doctrine with the title "Endless Conscious Torments," it does not sit well with many. For most, "hell" implies all that is understood according to the prevalent doctrine of postmortem judgment. In other words, when most people hear or say "hell," they are referring to ECT. However, this term should not include any details beyond its most basic rendering: the place or state of being created for Satan and fallen angels.[9] It has been established that hell also serves as the place of residence for those who die in their sins. Any details beyond these are not necessarily legitimate annotations. Neither has a consensus been drawn on whether or not hell is a state of being, a physical place with literal flames, or otherwise.

Linguistic Evolution

Many of the words that we use each day have been victims of the linguistic evolutionary process. If we did not know any better, dictionaries printed as little as fifty years ago would appear to contain words that were misdefined. Likewise, if we were to miraculously unearth a dictionary printed fifty years ahead of our time, similar discoveries would certainly occur.[10]

Consider the following list of terms that evidence the linguistic evolutionary process: "let"—to prevent; "abandon"—to subdue; "deduce"—to lead; "afford"—to advance; "match"—the wick of a candle or lamp; "bimbo"—a tough guy; "girl"—a young person/child (of either sex); "doom"—to decree; and "grin"—a scowl. The list goes on.

Even though many believe certain things about hell, the term, in and of itself, does not necessarily include any details beyond the basic description given above. Other details may describe it accurately, but those details cannot be included in its definition regardless of how much you or I agree with them. Definitions can only include what is indubitable.

For example, the unequivocal definition of a bridge is "a structure carrying a pathway or roadway over a depression or obstacle."[11] Granted, the word could evolve over several decades, but as long as certain details are equivocal, they should not be included in its definition. Although grammar and orthodoxy are subject to change, and although the term for postmortem judgment has been around for nearly two millennia, the concept has not, at

---

9. Matt 25:41.

10. The identifiable differences throughout outdated dictionaries range from details as insignificant as jots and titles to a metamorphosis so indicative that to deny their transformation would be equivalent to denying the apparent relativity of lexical nuances.

11. This definition is taken from Merriam-Webster's Dictionary.

any point in history, been indisputably understood down to the very last minutiae. The orthodox doctrine of postmortem judgement is, and always will be, the "correct opinion" of its day. Nevertheless, the "correct opinion" does not arbitrate absolute fact or even a proper definition. The definition of hell can only be delineated as far as all three classes of thought can agree, which does not currently amount to more than a few essential particulars.

Consider the following illustration: The sun has a very specific definition. As we learn more about it, we can include more details in its definition. In the year 1000 BCE, the human race understood cosmology on a much smaller scale. Three thousand years ago, the definition for the sun was understandably underdeveloped. While the sun has not changed much in three thousand years, its definition has changed much more so. The sun is obviously unaffected by our understanding of it. Likewise, our definition of the sun is not automatically affected by its intricacies. A definition can only inch closer to properly representing an object as we, as a whole, become more familiar with its intricacies.

The relationship between the definition and reality of hell mirrors the same linguistic standard. Although hell is not affected by our definition of it, neither is our definition of hell automatically affected by its intricacies. Each individual class of thought has introduced certain details into the discussion of hell which the other classes are not willing to accept. Therefore, we should not insert those ideas into its official definition.

Historically, the Christian family consisted of three separate schools of thought regarding postmortem judgment. Each school accepted, and continues to accept, the essential truths of the Faith. While each school has its own intricate understanding of hell, Christianity has one simple unadorned definition. Theoretically, this should leave room for us to disagree without casting stones. We all know how that goes, though.

Christian Universalism

Unfortunately, Unitarian Universalism has tainted the term "universalism" in the eyes of the Church at large. Businesses often struggle due to a similar effect their competitors sometimes have on terms that affect their industry. Every company strives to reach a point in their field where their trademark automatically comes to mind when their target audience says or reads certain terms that generally represent a wide variety of products or ideas. Coca-Cola Inc. is the epitome of such a brand. "Coke" has essentially replaced "soda" in certain areas of America. As they bask in their dominance—effortlessly absorbing its beneficial effects—other soda companies suffer from their monopoly on the general term for their product. Likewise, Christian Universalism suffers from a similar dominance Unitarian Universalism has on the term "universalism."

Due to the effect UU has on the term "universalism," Christian Universalists have a much larger obstacle to hurdle than do advocates of ECT or CI. At the very mention of the term, UU is the first thing that comes to mind for the masses, both within and beyond the Church. Few seem to realize that "universalism" was originally a Christian term that did not conflict with Christian presuppositions.

The doctrine of Universal Reconciliation basically affirms that everyone who dies without washing their robes in the uncontaminated blood of Jesus will have to stand before the judgment seat of Christ to give an account for everything they have done, whether good or bad. Without Jesus as their Mediator, they must endure judgment from God, who does not find joy in afflicting humankind,[12] but is purposeful with his affliction: "For the Lord will not cast off forever. Though he causes grief, yet he will show compassion according to the multitude of his mercies."[13] Jesus came to save us from the present perfect consequence of sin—spiritual death/disunity. CU affirms the greater hope of UR, which does not suggest that everyone is saved, as its skeptics might try to convey. Rather, it proclaims that God *will* accomplish his plan to restore creation as a whole, with respect to our ability to either accept or reject his Son.

The Savior of the world came to save *the* world from the wages of sin and to reunite us with he who first loved us. By rejecting the Remedy for our spiritual condition, many passively choose to take the much more difficult road to recovery. God kills to make alive and destroys to make way for restoration. Our Creator is just. He cannot remain impartial by limiting his grace to those privileged enough to come to their senses before they die. He who knew no sin became sin for the entire world. He died, left sin in the grave, became the first born from the dead,[14] is drawing those for whom he died[15] to himself,[16] and is therefore fulfilling his plan for creation—which has been identified, by Paul, as the mystery of his will.

Most people equate universalism with the belief that Jesus is *not* the only way to God—UU. This worldview has made its impression on the term mentioned, regardless of whether or not "Christian" precedes it.

---

12. Lam 3:33.
13. Lam 3:31–32.
14. Col 1:18.
15. That is, everyone.
16. John 12:32.

Believers respond just as they should against the connotation Unitarianism has branded on universalism. I was a Christian for nearly fifteen years without hearing a single word spoken about CU. While this chapter is dedicated to merely describing each school of thought, I will soon deliver the main course—course by course. Before then, I have one more doctrine to introduce.

Annihilation/Conditional Immortality

This doctrine and CU have something in common—neither is the orthodox view. However, those who accept CI enjoy something that Christian Universalists do not. Even though those who accept ECT reject both doctrines, they are far more sympathetic toward the doctrine that says God will annihilate the unrepentant than they are toward the doctrine that says God will eventually save everyone. I have my theories about why one paradigm is not equally sympathetic toward both alternatives, but I will save that for the appropriate chapter.

The doctrine of Conditional Immortality claims that everyone who dies without washing their robes in the uncontaminated blood of Jesus will have to stand before the judgment seat of Christ to give an account for everything they have done, whether good or bad. Without Jesus as their Mediator, they must endure judgment from God, who does not find joy in afflicting humankind, but is purposeful in his retribution by eventually annihilating the unrepentant as the final act of justice.[17] It reinforces Scripture by affirming that the wrath of God will be "drained to the dregs."[18] However, the condemned will experience each drop, in its fullness, until God determines that enough is enough.

The following will continue until the final drop of his wrath has fallen upon each wretched soul: the flame, pain, agony, grief, sorrow, thirst, heartache, a sense of loss, regret, cravings for all things desirable, including sleep, food, water, love, warmth, coolness, companionship, renewal, reconciliation, restoration, rest—relief. The intensity of each agony will "never" lessen *until* each soul is extinguished. Only then will God show mercy in giving them rest from their suffering, albeit via a lack of postmortem consciousness. Jesus was born to save *many* from this fate. When people reject Christ, they passively choose this *nearly* hopeless fate.[19] God cannot remain impartial by

---

17. Matt 10:28.

18. Ps 75:8.

19. Annihilation is "nearly" hopeless because while there is no hope of reconciliation, there is hope for the cessation of pain and suffering.

saving any out of hell or by snatching anyone out of the fire. Although, he will not damn anyone to ECT because his mercies are new *every* morning.[20] Jesus paid the ultimate price to save us from utter destruction.

Since CI is one of the three views of hell, I will attempt to allude to it here and there as I address the primary concerns of this book. A friend of mine had a paradigm shift around the same time as mine. The difference between the two of us was that he believed in CI before he considered CU. He now possesses great hope in UR. I do have somewhat of a bone to pick with CI, but that bone deserves a dish of its own.

---

20. Lam 3:22–23.

Section 2

Lifting the Veil

According to traditional writing styles, authors rarely dedicate anything beyond a relatively abrupt introduction to prepare the reader for an entire book's worth of chapters. Originally, I was going to follow this trend until I realized that the content of the first section was far too lengthy to cram into a single introductory chapter. Since this section begins the main course of this book, it will focus on the subject matter that is necessary to prepare you for the next section. As I address some discrepancies within the prevalent doctrine of postmortem judgement, I will attempt to refrain from addressing what I believe validates CU. I may briefly mention CI, but it will not occupy the main content of any chapter. This section will be about little more than that to which most Christians cling—ECT.

It is incontestable, on philosophical grounds, that everyone has some sort of an opinion about everything with which they are mindful. The instance we become cognizant of any given subject—even if it is just enough to avert obliviousness—we immediately form some kind of judgment about its validity and applicability in our lives. Even if we have not determined what we believe about it in an absolute sense, a judgment will have already begun to develop. As time passes, our understanding of the concept gradually matures until it has proven whether or not it is worthy of *our* acceptance.

Once we accept one idea as the most probable view, its mere existence almost seems to argue against alternate ideas. If it was unreliable, would we accept it as the most probable view? Perhaps, but who would admit to making a habit out of accepting false views? We believe *the* truth. Therefore, it goes without saying that alternate views must be in error—does it not? Regardless of how accurately other ideas may answer any of our questions, our "convictions" about these questions tend to produce a comfortable and secure feeling of certainty, which reinforces our commitment to those views. Even though doubt is widely viewed as a weakness and a detriment to a life of faith, I would like to suggest that doubt can be healthy aspect of the Christian faith.

This section approaches the prevalent doctrine of postmortem judgment in light of the following idea. Anyone who accepts ECT, or any other view, will rarely consider an alternate position unless they feel like they have a good reason to doubt what they believe. If a Christian believes that ECT is essential to their faith, why would they consider anything else? I have spoken with many believers who appeal to "special revelation" in defense of their theological convictions. They honestly believe that their beliefs about such things are indisputable because they are convinced that the Holy Spirit has "revealed" the truth to them. Regardless of how tempting it is to address this subject here, this portion of Section 2 cannot afford it the fair treatment that it is due. Therefore, I am postponing its analysis until the appropriate chapter.

In one way or another, nearly everything in this world can be compared or contrasted with anything else. For example, consider the relationship between an average couple. For the sake of this analogy, let's assume that most couples are decent and respectable human beings, each of whom genuinely desires what is best for the other. Given what we know about healthy relationships, it is safe to assume that few, if any, would suddenly abandon their partner or pursue a relationship with someone else unless they discovered that their partner was unfaithful.[1] Similarly, it is safe to assume that few, if any, would suddenly abandon their theological convictions unless they discovered that those beliefs were unreliable.

I am prepared to give those who accept the doctrine of ECT the benefit of doubt. Surely the majority of these believers genuinely believe that their convictions are faithful to Scripture and to the God-ordained laws of logic.[2] I certainly did. I would never have given CU, or any other doctrine, a fair hearing if I did not come to believe that my convictions about hell did not coincide with biblical teachings and God-given reason. The purpose of this section is to explain why I have come to believe as I do and to help you put your beliefs to the test as you consider the repercussions of ECT.

---

1. Everything has its exception, but this is generally the case.

2. This excludes those who mistakenly use Isaiah 55:8 to argue that biblical truths do not have to correspond with the laws of logic.

3

Heretically Orthodox Faith

A dog barks when his master is attacked. I would be a coward if I saw that God's truth is attacked and yet would remain silent.

—JOHN CALVIN

THE CHRISTIAN FAITH IS uniquely centered around faith. From that point outward, other Christian concepts branch out. Salvation results from faith in Christ. Therefore, Christianity is not primarily about salvation. It is rooted in faith in Christ. If the Christian religion was initially about salvation, then it would primarily be about obtaining the free ticket into heaven that is supposedly required when we die and is unavailable thereafter. However, Jesus did not die to save us from some future event, but to restore our relationship with God here and now. He came to save us from something presently. He rose from the dead so that we may have life today and to have it abundantly, which transfers into life hereafter. When he returns, he expects a bride that is full of life and vitality, rather than one that is lethargic and on the brink of death. Christians should be preparing for his momentous return.

One of the most admirable things about the Church is how committed she is to remaining unblemished for her bridegroom. Even though that is a healthy aspiration for the Church, there is an Achilles Heel that accompanies her unquenchable thirst for doctrinal piety. Her insatiable hunger in this regard is the result of her obsessive desire to identify with the first-century church of Laodicea, which was the only church about whom Jesus had *nothing* negative to say.[1] Even though she is accepted as she is, should she not long for her bridegroom to say, "I find no fault within you"?

A doctorate in horticulture is not required for anyone to understand that a tree which fails to yield fruit in season is as good as dead. Likewise,

---

1. Rev 3:14–22.

a doctorate in theology is not required for anyone to understand that faith which fails to yield fruit is of no use.[2] Jesus did not hide how he felt about the spiritual condition of "lukewarm" Christians.[3] We should be either hot or cold, because Jesus said he *will* spew the lukewarm out of his mouth. In candid terms, he would rather we be anti-Christ than to take his name in vain by lacking the fruit of authenticity.

On the other hand, a lack of fruit does not necessarily equate inauthenticity. Any number of factors can account for a Christian's apparent fruitlessness. It could be that the fruit is "out of season". One's expectations could be too high or even premature. After seasons of pruning, the branch may simply be genetically unable to blossom. Christians long to be involved in God's plans for the world. When all is said and done, we long to be found faithful as we please our Maker by producing much fruit that stores up incorruptible riches in glory.[4]

For the utmost of his highest, church leaders have committed their entire lives to shepherding the body of Christ. Many fail to realize the enormous burden that comes along with this responsibility. Just as parents shield their children from potential harm, so too do church officials aim to protect the lambs of Christ. They invest much time and effort into preparing their flock for life outside of the walls of their church because stumbling blocks are just around every corner. There are so many different kinds of stumbling blocks that, even if pastors had all the time in the world, they could not fully prepare any single believer for the trials of this world—much less an entire congregation.

Nevertheless, they do the best they can. In order to make the best out of this situation, they have to focus on what matters the most. From their perspective, what could be more of a stumbling block for their flock than false doctrine? Resulting from the Christian desire to remain "hot" or doctrinally pure, many become cold toward their family-in-Christ. The Church seems to have a constant and incurable phobia of backsliding, which has, for some reason, become synonymous with liberal and unorthodox stances. In an attempt to avoid doctrinal impurity, many have strayed onto the broad path of comfortability, which has been found in prevalent/orthodox theological positions.[5]

---

2. Jas 2:26.

3. He was more concerned about the interior than the exterior because our exterior is directly affected by our interior.

4. Matt 6:20.

5. The orthodoxy of Catholicism places the authority of tradition on the same plane as the authority of Scripture. It also condones apostolic succession, which theoretically gives the pope apostolic authority. This ideology has crept into Protestant theology, as a

Childlike Faith

Faith is understood somewhat differently from person to person. Each person's comprehension of this subject is influenced by their worldview and may differ, to any degree, from another's. Any two people could easily accept the same worldview and disagree about the finer details of faith. Show me two theologians who accept the doctrine of ECT and I will show you two informed individuals who do not see eye to eye.[6] Since Christianity has more than one denomination, it is not surprising that there is no consensus on the intricacies of faith. There is room to disagree on the hues of the Faith without having any altercations over its color scheme.

Everyone possesses a set of lenses through which they interpret their worldview's portrait of reality. Each religion has a different canvas on which their worldview has been painted. The secular palette, for example, portrays faith as something that is blind. This worldview insists that faith is *a belief in something for which there is little to no compelling evidence.* Naturally, everyone understands each facet of reality as their worldview permits. At first glance, the childlike faith depicted in the Bible[7] appears to support the secularist's presuppositions. Children believe what they are told for the sake of belief. Their faith can, indeed, be understood as blind in the fullest expression of the term because they sincerely trust the source from which information usually comes—their loved ones.

Regardless of how faith appears to cynics, the Bible does not support the notion that saving faith is blind; at least, not entirely. Much like children, Christians sincerely trust in the source of their faith because they love God. Yet there is evidence which confirms that their childlike trust in God is not naïve, but reasonable. Stupid faith in random assertions may represent the secular definition of faith, but forcing a secular understanding on a scriptural concept is nothing more than a straw man fallacy.[8] The Bible defines its *own* terms, as does every other worldview.

When we interpret Scripture, it is important to acknowledge that it contains historical documents that were not written directly to a twenty-first-century audience.[9] If we desire to understand the intended message behind what is written, we have to make some attempt to read its words

---

wolf in sheep's clothing, branded as orthodoxy.

6. This is the case with every worldview.

7. Matt 18:3.

8. The "straw man" fallacy misrepresents an opposing position to make it easier to refute. Straw man arguments oversimplify opposing views or disregard inconvenient points in favor of points that are easier to argue against.

9. However, it remains applicable to anyone who has an ear to hear.

through the eyes of those to whom it was originally written. It is also important to realize that certain terms or phrases used in any historic document may not have the same implications when spoken in a modern context.

Innocent, trusting, and—yes—very naïve children *blindly* trust in their parents. Out of those three adjectives, one term is unlike the others. Even though the first two terms can be used negatively, they can also be used in a positive context. However, the third term is seldom, if ever, used in anything but a negative context. Have you ever attempted to use it in a positive context? Could you? It seems difficult to think of a single instance in which it could be used positively. Yet in the grand scheme of things, we are all just like naïve children tugging on the robe of our Heavenly Father. Is "naïve" a negative attribute in this context? People are, by nature, no less naïve when it comes to spirituality than a small child is oblivious to the dangers of life. The difference is in the object of our faith, rather than in an action out of context.

God, as the perfect father figure, would never lead us in the wrong direction. He is the most trustworthy of those worthy of trust. In most cases, earthly parents can relate to God in this aspect because they would likewise never *intentionally* mislead their children.[10] The difference between God and humanity pertains to intent. We are not omniscient. Our mental capacity is virtually handicapped in relation to God's, which often results in mistakes and regret. Regardless of how committed we are to giving our loved ones reliable guidance, we are bound to fail in one way or another. God, on the other hand, is not inadequate in any regard. He is perpetually trustworthy and absolutely reliable. Like our earthly parents, he loves all of his children and desires our faith. Unlike them, he also *deserves* our faith and is worthy of it.

Faith in an Interpretation

The doctrine of ECT is undoubtedly a complex doctrine. Few seem to understand its intricacies as thoroughly as they should. Many boldly condone ECT and passionately announce that their faith is securely placed in what the Bible "clearly teaches". Yet in doing so, they must also admit that they do not have a thorough understanding of certain biblical "mysteries" because the doctrine raises many difficult questions that the Bible apparently fails to address.

Most of those who accept ECT believe essentially the same thing about hell. Even though most typically accept a hyper-literalistic interpretation

---

10. There are always exceptions.

of the Bible's description of postmortem judgment, there are a few who do not interpret related passages as literally as others. The masses believe that the best interpretation of Scripture is a literal one, which is somewhat true. However, many fail to understand that the best interpretation is not just a literal one, but one that allows the context to determine the best method of interpretation.

As with any document, Scripture requires the interpreter to take numerous details into consideration before drawing any significant conclusions from its subject matter. Scripture was originally written to a specific group of people, who lived in a culture that was totally foreign to many of us. If we interpret these ancient documents without looking through their ancient lenses, we will inevitably end up with a disarray of relative interpretations.[11]

It is possible, I presume, that someone could properly interpret a portion of the Bible with little to no understanding of the culture of its original recipients. Plain essential truths are just that—essentially plain. However, when we view vague nonessential issues as though they are obvious and essentially true, we are all but asking for widespread confusion. This is precisely the conundrum in which many Christians place themselves, which leads to *necessary* appeals to mystery or ignorance in order to justify their acceptance of doctrines with apparent problematic premises. Consider the following list of questions that anyone should ask as they interpret the Bible:

1. To whom was the the document *originally* written?
2. How would its original audience understand it?
3. Are there any idioms that would have carried significant implications for *them*?
4. Did the author use any hyperbolic language in order to place emphasis on key points?
5. Should it be interpreted in light of related passages?
6. Is there any other figurative language used with which the original culture would be familiar?
7. How do other translations of the Bible, especially literal ones,[12] translate significant terms or phrases?

---

11. *Misreading Scripture with Western Eyes: Removing Cultural Blinders to Better Understand the Bible* by E. Randolph Richards and Brandon J. O'Brien is an excellent book on this subject; see Appendix D.

12. No translation of the Bible is literal in an absolute sense. Rather, some have been translated more literally than others.

8. Is each translation of value? If so, what purpose do they serve?

Jonathan K. Dodson wrote an excellent article entitled, "Questioning the Gospel." Although I do not necessarily agree or disagree with anything he believes, I believe his article can add more depth to the subject at hand. Although it is not necessary, I recommend that you take the time to read Appendix A before you finish reading the remaining portion of this chapter.

Apologia

In 2013, my wife and I attended a morning class at a local southern Baptist Church near our hometown. As the leader of this class was guiding us through the weekly lesson, he came to a certain point where he went off on a tangent. Since the leader of this class clearly had an interest in apologetics, I enjoyed the detour. Before I could get a word in edgewise, a lady, nearly on cue, began to give her testimony. She explained how much she had developed since she went through the Evangelism Explosion program. By the time she finished, she had, more or less, validated my observation about the Church's unnecessary dogmatism toward nonessential doctrines.[13]

She began by explaining how she was raised in a Christian home where she was taught what she was "supposed" to believe and how she was finally taught how to defend those beliefs. On the surface, her testimony sounded great. Yet as she continued, something felt amiss. After I had time to meditate on everything that was said in class I realized that she said nothing to affirm that she had ever *tested* what she was taught to believe and, later on, to defend. When she was taught how to defend what she was *told* to believe, she was, more or less, *told* how to do so rather than taught how to test the presuppositions behind her beliefs and others'.

Apologetics is a noteworthy hobby. Even if someone does not fully understand the intricacies of what they are defending, it is difficult to criticize them if they are witnessing to the uncommitted. However, there is a huge difference between defending the essential doctrines of the Faith without understanding their intricacies and defending nonessential doctrines without an understanding of them. Memorizing the "correct" thing to say about what we are taught to believe is much different than understanding why a certain position is the most plausible.[14]

---

13. Ignorance regarding the fluidity of orthodoxy is responsible for incessant dogmatism against anything that strays from prevalent presuppositions.

14. Skeptics know the difference between memorized answers and responses that have been tested tried and true.

I would never deny the wisdom in being familiar with the verses that may support one doctrine or contradict another. However, I do have a problem with proof-text argumentation because it can detract from our philosophical and theological maturity. It is far too easy to get caught up in searching the Bible to find anything that *might* support our presuppositions.[15] Proof-text argumentation is one of the most common stumbling blocks for Christians and skeptics alike because it can transform the Bible into a personal hammer to pound on the curious rather than an efficient tool to form, and maybe even transform, our current understanding of spiritual concepts.[16]

Cognitive Dissonance

This concept is technically described as a medical conflict that occurs when beliefs or assumptions are contradicted by new information. It was introduced by the psychologist Leon Festinger in the late 1950s. He, and later researchers, examined how most people, when confronted with new information that does not support their current understanding of the world, seek to preserve their convictions by convincing themselves that no conflict really exists.[17] Cognitive dissonance can account for sudden attitude change, which is frequently a result of discussing the subject matter at hand.

Obviously, CD does not discredit anyone's presuppositions. It simply explains why we reject things in the inexplicable ways that we do. CD is generally understood as a negative quality possessed by the uninformed, rather than a tendency with which everyone wrestles. Due to a poor understanding of its effect on everyone, some people suffer from its debilitating effects more than others; yet no one has a legitimate excuse for succumbing to it. Those who are committed to intellectual integrity must acknowledge its effect on themselves and prevent it from affecting their obligation to test all things.[18]

Conclusion

By the end of this chapter, I do not expect you to be ready to hear my case for CU. I have three more chapters to whet your appetite. The purpose of this

---

15. This is confirmation bias.

16. Refer to Appendix B for a list of verses, which is by no means exhaustive, that presumably support ECT.

17. This usually results in someone rejecting, explaining away, and/or avoiding new information.

18. 1 Thess 5:21.

chapter was for addressing how traditional[19] Christians seem to have placed their faith in the doctrine of ECT because of their longing to be known for trusting God's Word for what it "clearly says."[20] At first glance, I can understand why many believe the Bible supports that doctrine. I also understand how many can justify placing their faith in this teaching even though there are just as many passages that appear to teach something else entirely.

When I accepted this doctrine, I built my case for it on at least three premises: Premise 1—God is absolutely just. Premise 2—the Bible is inspired by God and is, therefore, absolutely authoritative. Premise 3—The Bible supports the doctrine of ECT. Conclusion—ECT is necessarily true and just. Moreover, since God has chosen to pursue justice in a way that does not make complete sense to *us*, the problem is with *our* understanding rather than with the Bible. Even though this argument seems reasonable, especially to those who accept premise 3, it is *not* reasonable because it requires an arbitrary appeal to mystery.[21] It discredits God-ordained logical laws and undermines other biblical teachings that support rationality. God encourages us to *come and reason with him*.[22] He commands us to *test all things*.[23] If something does not seem to make sense, that is likely because it is not sensible.

Premise 1 is essentially true, on philosophical grounds. Premise 2 is necessarily true according to the Christian worldview. Yet premise 3 is subject to interpretation. Therefore, it could be untrue. Christians have to stop treating nonessential premises like they are pillars of the Christian Faith. If God wanted us to blindly believe what we are told to believe or what the Bible *seems* to teach, even in the midst of contradiction, he would not have commanded us to test all things and to reason them out *with* him. If Christians place their faith in prevalent presuppositions and refuse to test contradictory concepts that are dear to them, we might as well accept the secularist's definition of faith as blind and unreasonable—only to justify irrationality with an appeal to mystery. God forbid.

The next three chapters will focus on four of God's attributes, each of which have an immediate effect on the biblical concept of postmortem judgment. Each chapter will place ECT's portrayal of those attributes under the microscope, reveal how they must be understood in light of that doctrine, and prepare the reader to consider that which ECT conditions believers to reject.

---

19. I consider myself a traditionalist in most aspects.

20. This is the fallacy of reification: the Bible does not *say* anything. It requires an interpreter.

21. An appeal to mystery is only fallacies when it is arbitrary.

22. Isa 1:18.

23. 1 Thess 5:21.

4

Expiring Grace and Mercy

> You cannot out-sin the grace of God! And if he expects me to forgive my enemy over and over and over with no limitation on it, then listen to this: If God put any limitation on his grace you and I would be greater than God when it came to forgiveness. And we know that's not true.
>
> —CHARLES STANLEY

ON DECEMBER 31, 1999, the final seconds of the century were coming to a close. Better yet the last few seconds of the millennium were ticking down as a good portion of the world anxiously embraced their loved ones and hoped against hope that all would be well. Many expected the worst, while others were prepared for doomsday. The apocalypse had all but arrived and there was nothing anyone could do but countdown its arrival. When the clock struck midnight, there was a deafening silence throughout the cosmos.

***

Hollywood, along with some assistance from the media and other outlets, successfully convinced the general public that Y2K was the beginning of the end. From hindsight, many felt naïve once it was evident that the ball had dropped. Others prided themselves on their skepticism and rubbed it in everyone's faces for some time afterward.

Our perception of reality plays a significant role in each of our lives. Throughout our days, we make choices that are influenced by certain factors that seem to be out of our control. Although many of these factors are determined by our worldview, they are not entirely beyond our control.

Everyone's worldview affects how they respond to propaganda, like that of Y2K, just as it affects their reactions toward superstitions like those behind the Mayan calendar's end-time prophecy.

Although each person's worldview seems to be engrained in their personhood, neural plasticity has revealed that we are not enslaved to our systems of belief or to the choices that we have made. Throughout the latter portion of my life, there have been a few significant shifts in my understanding of several theological systems that most traditionalists[1] consider more essential to the Faith than they ought. Many Christians, both laymen and evangelicals alike, have blurred the lines between what is essential to authentic Christianity and what is not.

C. Michael Patton addresses evangelical Christians as follows: "Evangelicals: We can and we must distinguish between essentials and non-essentials better. Draw our circles too tightly, and we slip into fundamentalism.[2] Draw our circles too wide, and we slip into liberalism."[3] In his article, he suggests that many do not seem to understand that every doctrine that is currently accepted as orthodox is not as high on the theological totem pole as those that are essential to the Christian faith.[4] Before you continue any further in this chapter, I highly recommend that you read his article.

***

As you know, I accepted the traditional doctrine of postmortem judgment for the majority of my Christian life. I am well aware of the fact that those who accept ECT have no desire to devalue the grace and mercy of God. Actually, most would scoff at any statement that intentionally limits God's attributes—as they should. They rightly proclaim, from the rooftops, that God's grace and mercy is, indeed, new *every* morning.[5]

Although the title of this chapter may seem to suggest otherwise, I would never suggest that those who accept ECT see God's grace and mercy as something that is expiring. Therefore, any offense taken at the title of this

---

1. For the record, I am a traditionalist in many areas of theology.

2. I also consider myself a fundamentalist, for the most part.

3. C. Michael Patton, "Evangelicals: We Can and Must Distinguish Between Essentials and Non-Essentials Better," *Credo House* (blog), October 8, 2010, http://www.reclamingthemind.org/blog/2010/10/evangelicals-we-can-and-we-must-distinguish-between-essentials-and-non-essentials-better/.

4. I am referring to what, if taken away, would de-Christianize Christianity.

5. Lam 3:22–23. New, that is, up to the morning in which there will be no more night. His grace and mercy will be perpetually fresh, forevermore.

chapter is unjustified. It would only be justified if I was implying anything that misrepresents their motives or beliefs. Since I am not suggesting that they *believe* that God's grace and mercy is expiring, it would be wise to ask, "What would be an alternate purpose for the title of this chapter?" In order to discover the answer to that question, one should ask, "What is the goal of this section?"

The Theological Pivot

Ultimately, it all boils down to what we deem the pivotal point of the matter, for which there are only two options: *Either the validity of ECT determines whether or not God's grace and mercy are immutable, or the immutability of his grace and mercy determines whether or not ECT is valid.* One of these concepts is a necessary doctrine in the Christian faith and only one can be true since the two are mutually exclusive.

When I accepted ECT, the idea that its premises may reduce to absurdity was just as foreign to me as it currently is to anyone else. If we take the Christian stance that affirms the inerrancy of Scripture, we must also affirm that none of its teachings are fallacious in any way. Therefore, when we come across a doctrine that fails in one way or another, we have to doubt the validity of that doctrine or appeal to mystery. Cognitive dissonance causes many to lean more toward the latter.

Reductio ad absurdum[6]

We, as members of one body, are familiar with God's attributes, all of which have been revealed through special and general revelation—Scripture and nature, respectively. As Christians, we acknowledge that God is full of grace and overflowing with mercy. We accept the authority of Scripture as special revelation when it describes his character. We do not struggle with what the Bible says about the grace and mercy of God and its newness *every* morning.[7] On the other hand, there is dissension among us regarding what that actually means.

---

6. *Reductio ad absurdum* is the technique of reducing an argument or hypothesis to absurdity, by pushing the argument's premises or conclusions to their logical limits and showing how ridiculous the consequences would be, thus disproving or discrediting the argument.

7. Lam 3:22–23.

A Blessing, Yet a Curse

How would you feel if one of your doctrinal convictions portrayed divine grace and mercy as a blessing for some, but a curse for many more? What if I told you that the theoretical expiration date of these attributes does just that? It almost feels impious to suggest, even hypothetically, that God's grace and mercy could be a curse for anyone. However, if prevalent presuppositions prevail, we cannot avoid this conclusion. It is understandably difficult for anyone to acknowledge that a doctrine that they have accepted for the majority of their Christian life reduces to this absurdity.[8] Yet according to ECT, this expiration date is ever looming in the shadows, ultimately revealing it as a curse in disguise, a wolf in sheep's clothing.

If ECT turns out to be true, the eternal gospel[9] is not good news for *all people*,[10] but very bad news for most of us. To the surprise of many, ECT and CU teach the same thing about God's attributes up to the point of death. However, ECT distinguishes itself by implying that *death* is the most significant event in our lives. Since it places more emphasis on death than it should, it suggests that there is a spiritual law of entropy of sorts, which pushes God's attributes toward a date of expiration that is relative to the life of each of us.

ECT presumes that there are no "second chances" after death. Although it may sound like a brash assertion, I doubt that anyone would have ever made this claim if they properly understood another concept—final judgment. Anyone who accepts the authority of Scripture cannot deny this concept. However, its intricacies are not as cut and dried as many presuppose. The majority of the Christians with whom I have conversed read far too much into the word "final" than they should. If I am correct, presupposing that there are no opportunities for grace or mercy beyond the grave is detrimental to a proper exegesis of Scripture.

Why do so many Christians believe that there is no postmortem hope for the lost? Before we seek an answer to that question, beyond merely saying, "Because the Bible says so," or claiming that it would eliminate any motivation to seek salvation here and now, we should ask, "What exactly would no one get another chance at?" Salvation? If so, from what? Postmortem judgment? If so, I agree. The Bible states, "It is appointed for man to die

---

8. This is especially so with passages such as Luke 2:10, which says the birth of Christ is good news for all people. Granted, the Calvinist would say it is only good news for "all kinds of people."

9. Rev 14:6.

10. Luke 2:10.

once, and after that comes judgment."[11] This verse is frequently used as a proof-text for ECT, but many fail to realize that it says nothing about the duration of the punishment. Rather, its emphasis is on *the matter of factness* of judgement.

The following verse implicitly sheds some light on this subject. "So, Christ, having been offered once to bear the sins of many, will appear a second time, not to deal with sin but to save those who are eagerly waiting for him."[12] This verse parallels Christ's death with ours. It implies that bodily death occurs once. Furthermore, it affirms the eventual "dealing with" of sin. It is obvious that Jesus saves those who are in him. It is also obvious that those who die outside of Christ are not saved. Scripture teaches that those who "pass away" before they have been grafted into the vine will be cast into the fire. However, the Bible is not very descriptive when it comes to what that entails.

Some traditionalists who believe in ECT disagree with others who believe that grace is no longer available for anyone who dies in their sins. Although they cling to the prevalent doctrine of postmortem judgment, they believe the availability of God's grace and mercy never ceases, that it is eternally available to *all* who need it. However, they also believe that they will never be drawn to Christ.

In an attempt to justify their stance, they reason something like this: *Since the Bible affirms that ECT is true and that God's grace is new every morning, those who die unsaved will never believe in Christ.* Since the Bible does not teach that anyone will, or even can, reject the grace of God forever, those who claim otherwise must give a logical explanation for *why* it is true rather than merely projecting *that* it is so. Many attempt to use proof-text arguments in their defense, which merely consists of quoting Bible verses without explaining how they support this presupposition, as though their interpretation is the only possible one. Any reference to "a hardening of hearts" is usually enough for many.

In a realm where everyone ceaselessly rejects the grace of God and are willfully unrepentant, it logically follows that their rebellion is sustained by he who created them and their current residence. In other words, if ECT is true, God is ultimately responsible for sustaining the rebellion of the unrepentant. This is the primary dilemma that many Calvinists wrestle with

---

11. Heb 9:27.
12. Heb 9:28.

as they attempt to deny double predestination,[13] even though that logically follows from their presuppositions.[14]

Many who take this position claim that the hearts of those in hell will be so hardened that they will forever despise the grace and mercy of God. Theoretically, postmortem suffering continuously hardens the hearts of the "forsaken". Even though we can easily envision such a scenario, there is no biblical support for it. It is purely a philosophical position that does not stand firmly against scrutiny, which is something it is rarely subject to within the church. If hell or the lake of fire continuously hardens those who are trapped within its clutches, its Architect is ultimately responsible for what happens beyond the rhetorical line he has drawn in the sand.[15]

The Bible explicitly declares that God is the Creator of *all things*, which includes the chambers of hell. It also declares that *everything* that God created was created *good*.[16] If the former is true, God is responsible for hell's effect on those who writhe in its flames because he *designed* it to have whatever effect it has on its residents. If we are correct about God's omnibenevolence, then we should take the Bible seriously when it says that *it is not his will for any to perish but for all to come to repentance*. Granted, it does not say, "Therefore, none will perish"—but neither does it say, "All who perish can/will never be saved."

What if God actually created hell with a good purpose in mind for its inhabitants? Could we expect such a thing from the God we know? David sings in the Psalms, "His judgments are to be desired more than fine gold, even much fine gold; sweeter also than honey and drippings of the honeycomb."[17] Is the eternal torment of the uncommitted "sweet"?

Image a scenario in which grace and mercy remains available until the very last soul is drawn to the cross. You have, just now, created a world in your mind that is better than the one God created—that is, if ECT is true. The seemingly automated response to all of this goes something like this: "We don't have to wonder. God has *clearly* revealed what hell is like. Whether we like it or not, that's just the way it is. We don't fully understand his plans. One day, when we are glorified and made complete in Christ,

---

13. Double predestination teaches that God not only elects certain people to receive grace, but he also chooses who will go to hell.

14. Some Calvinists do not deny double predestination, but try to accommodate it alongside human responsibility.

15. That is, the moment of death/the final beat of the heart.

16. I cannot help but remember the hymn that repeatedly states, "God makes all things beautiful, in his time."

17. Ps 19:10.

these things will be revealed. We will find joy in his perfect plan for creation. We will find great joy in knowing he has brought justice to the world."

That was roughly my response to anyone who challenged my belief in ECT. When I accused skeptics of letting their emotions get in the way of their judgment, I believed that I was being perfectly reasonable. It took me a long time to realize that my heart had hardened toward anything that opposed my interpretation of related passages or philosophical presuppositions. It took even longer for me to realize that I was just as guilty of letting my emotions interfere with my judgement as anyone else.

Properly Determining Negative Counterparts

According to the Bible, what is salvation all about? If we were to ask this question to a random group of Christians, we would receive a variety of answers. To ensure their reliability, we would need to poll each person privately to prevent one answer from influencing another. Different forms of this question would emphasize different aspects of salvation, which could produce several responses from each person. It would be wise to ask this question in numerous ways in order to receive a thorough response.

Historically, the church has taught that we are saved *from* our sin. However, at no point in history have we been able to draw a consensus on what that means. Scripture does not address this concept as clearly as many presume because we have focused far too much on the negative aspect of salvation than we have on the positive. The gospel is not something we accept because of some negativity or another. It is *good tidings to all people*, rather than something we "better accept or else." Although there are negative consequences for dying in our sins, the Bible's depiction of salvation does not focus primarily on those things. Scripture always portrays salvation in a superlative light rather than in a shadow. In short, Scripture concentrates more on eternal life and its correlation with salvation, while it merely alludes to its counterpart.

Eternal life is defined once in the entirety of Scripture: "And this is eternal life—that they know you the only true God, and Jesus Christ whom you have sent."[18] This is the only passage that makes any attempt to define eternal life, which parallels salvation. Surprisingly, it says nothing about its duration, beyond the supposed implication of the term that is usually associated with time—eternal. I am not attempting to place any limitation on the duration of "knowing God." Other passages and philosophical propositions ensure the irrevocability and eternality of life in Christ. Nevertheless,

---

18. John 17:3.

the only passage that defines eternal life does not place emphasis on its duration, but on its nature—relationship.

Currently, Christians are experiencing eternal/*aiōnion* life, albeit only as a taste of what is to come.[19] Likewise, unbelievers are experiencing eternal/ *aiōnion* condemnation[20] here and now,[21] yet only as a taste of what is to come. All who are in Christ intimately know God just as he knows them. All who are not in Christ have never known him, nor he them.[22]

Many presume that since *aiōnion* life is unending, *aiōnion* comdemnation must reflect its counterpart. This is partly drawn from a certain interpretation of the sheep and goats parable.[23] I have to admit that this parable is staggering for anyone on either side of the eschatological fence. Although I once interpreted it through lenses that were tinted with prevalent presuppositions, and therefore saw those presuppositions woven throughout it, I no longer believe the parable was intended to portray what is generally read between its lines. Obviously, I have discarded my old lenses.

Many have a difficult time understanding how hell passages can be taken seriously apart from the doctrine of ECT. Since my defection, I have been accused of many things—one of which has been of not taking the Bible seriously. Jesus warned those who flocked around him, as starving sheep without a shepherd, that it is better for people to live their entire lives maimed[24] than to be thrown into the hell[25] of fire/to experience postmortem judgment. In light of this passage, and others like it, there was a time when I could not imagine how this warning could remain undiluted apart from an endless rendering of postmortem suffering.

Consider how I once interpreted this passage: *The sheep, which represent Christians, are awarded "eternal life," while the goats, which represent unbelievers, are awarded an "eternal punishment." Since the word "eternal" is the adjective of the life received and the punishment given, it must reflect equally on each subject.* Up to this point, my beliefs have not changed. My reasoning continued: *Since "eternal" refers to duration, and since we know that life in Christ is endless, the punishment/consequence for a lack of faith must also be endless.* This is where my beliefs have changed. If "eternal" refers to the endlessness of life, I would have to agree with the traditional view—even

---

19. "Jesus knows me, this I love."
20. That is, the wrath of God.
21. John 3:18.
22. This does not mean in a salvific sense; I will write more on this later.
23. Matt 25:31–46.
24. Matt 18:8.
25. That is, "Gehenna."

though it would conflict with the Greek word for "punishment." The Greek word for "punishment" effects its adjective more than I once thought.

In this passage, "punishment" is translated from the Greek term *kolasis*. Many have argued that its etymological roots are in the field of horticulture, which would imply that it is meant for correction rather than pure retribution. William Barclay has noted that "there is no instance in Greek secular literature where kolasis does not mean remedial punishment." Since there has been some dispute with this study, I will not push it any further than is necessary.

Kolasis has a non-identical twin sibling. Meet the brother of kolasis—timōria. The only difference between the two is that the latter has absolutely no corrective nuances. It would be a stretch to suggest that those who penned the New Testament were unfamiliar with their differences. If its penmen were not meaning to suggest that postmortem judgment was remedial, why would they use a term that has *corrective* connotations when there was one at their disposal that did not?

This lone detail did not cause me to set my sail away from the prevailing current of orthodoxy, but it was one of the greater winds on my voyage. There are many other theological considerations beyond the two highlighted in this chapter that need to be considered in light of ECT, most of which will be examined soon enough.

5

Deficient Love

God loves each of us as if there were only one of us.
—ST. AUGUSTINE

Is that so? Does God love every decedent of Adam as if they were the only ones to love? Or is his love reserved for those who place their faith in Christ *before* they die? Did Augustine mean that God loves each *Christian* as though there was only one to love? Which rendition of Augustine's statement is scripturally and logically coherent? I believe a solid case can be given in favor of God's unfailing love *all* people. He *is* Love, after all.

Few in any camp would dare to suggest that God fails to love all of humanity in some measure. Therefore, Christians are prone to respond positively to claims like Augustine's without verbalizing the implications of their doctrinal convictions. However, when we realize how the inclusivity of God's love affects our doctrinal presuppositions, many prefer to challenge its inclusivity rather than their presuppositions.[1]

Scripture instructs us to beware of anyone who teaches doctrines that are anti-Christ. "A tickling of the ears"[2] is often associated with such teachings. Since it is within our nature to allow our emotions to get the best of us, Christians often have to remind themselves that Scripture ultimately determines the validity of doctrinal claims. Although Scripture holds authority over our "feelings", Christians have been given a new spirit that bears witness to the truth and even unbelievers have been gifted with a conscience that bears witness to spiritual truths that are hidden throughout the natural

---

1. Note: When there is friction between God's attributes and our presuppositions, we should question our presuppositions rather than the inclusive nature of God's love, grace, mercy, etc.

2. 2 Tim 4:3.

world.[3] Therefore, what some dismiss as a fallacious appeal to the emotions very well may be a legitimate appeal to the conscience.

In defense of ECT, many say that "God is love, but he is also just." This response is religiously parroted as though God's justice *relies* on a sentencing of ECT. In the minds of many, it also justifies their decision to ignore alternate doctrinal possibilities.[4] Similar insecurities can be seen in people who judge their peers by their appearance. It does not take a licensed psychologist to realize that people behave similarly because they are dissatisfied with something about themselves.[5]

A large portion of the Church has been convinced that if anyone believes the love of God will eventually result in the reconciliation of all things, which is an explicit decree of the Most High,[6] then they must have either overlooked God's justice or intentionally ignored it. It was not that long ago when I made similar assumptions. I recall feeling a sense of obligation toward anyone whose beliefs did not correspond with my own.

Although I may have thought quite differently at the time, I cannot say that I believed as I did because the Bible left me no other options. I was committed to my belief in ECT because I was convinced that Scripture taught that it was the only *just* consequence for dying in one's sins—not to mention that it was the only teaching that was condoned by any church I had ever attended. I revered the written word of God, accepted its authority, and trusted that the Holy Spirit was guiding my interpretation of it.

When I accepted ECT, I reasoned that since the Bible taught this doctrine then it had to be just. Since I believed that the Bible was inerrant, if ECT *appeared* illogical then the problem was with "human reasoning,"[7] rather than with the Bible. Those were the only options, as far as I knew—ECT was necessarily valid.

Before I became a Christian Universalist, there were several passages that prevented me from outright accepting the doctrine. I was hopeful in my Christian Universalism for a couple months before I was persuaded through my studies. Passages such as those that mention souls being in torment in the lake of fire "forever and ever" were hindrances that could not have been honestly ignored.

---

3. Rom 2:15.

4. Again, this opinion stems from when I believed similarly.

5. This can also be seen when someone attempts to make others feel uneducated or ignorant due to their own intellectual insecurities.

6. Col 1:19–20.

7. I will return to this point later.

If Christians would have the decency to give the benefit of doubt to those who believe differently, we would be able to avoid unnecessary diversions in our quest for the truth. We should not assume that others are necessarily not as genuine as we are simply because they believe differently. More times than not, people have faulty presuppositions rather than a disingenuous personality.

A Threefold Chord

When three cords are intertwined, they become one and are considered qualitatively inseparable. Even though anyone could untwine a cord, that action would be detrimental to its worth/resilience. Just as a cord with three strands cannot be easily broken, neither can the threefold chord of divine love be easily broken.[8] Unlike a physical cord, the transcendent chord of God's love has always been one. If it was possible to "untwine" this chord, it would devolve into a fragmented representation of perfection—an imperfect kind of love—one that may be acceptable for humankind, but is unacceptable for, and unworthy of, God.

The English language is largely to blame for our limited understanding of the love of God. If we are sincerely interested in understanding what the Bible has to say about anything, we have to have some knowledge of the languages in which it was originally written.[9] Since the English language has only one word to represent many kinds of love, English translators of the Bible were at a disadvantage when they came across different Greek/Hebrew words for love. If we fail to acknowledge this fact, or if we refuse to acknowledge its importance, we cannot hope to read the Bible for all that it is worth.[10]

The Bible expresses love through three Greek words, each of which emphasizes three distinct concepts: *agapē* (ἀγάπη), *erōs* (ἔρως), and *philia* (φιλία). When each word, in its pristine form, is integrated with the others, they form the inseparable threefold chord of God's unfailing love. In order to grasp the heights and depths of God's love for us, let's briefly touch on the meaning of each term.

Agapē. This form of love seems to suffice when we think of the unconditional nature of God's love. If we know *anything* about God, we know

---

8. Eccl 4:12.

9. We can rely only so much on translators since they have presuppositions like everyone else.

10. This is just one of many handicaps that can constrain our understanding of the Bible.

that his love for creation is unimaginably vast and absolutely unconditional. Of the three, *agapē* is arguably the most "God-like." Unfortunately, this is the only term that many consider when they think of the love of God. Of course, no one can understand the intricacies of his love perfectly, but we can develop a better understanding of it if we reach beyond one Greek term. I am not trying to degrade agapē, but anything less than a full description of the love of God cheapens that which is of infinite worth.

Erōs. This form of love is usually associated with eroticism. Although we usually associate *erōs* with sexuality, it can be experienced outside of a provocative relationship. It can be seen as a higher quality of love than that for which *philia* can account and a lower quality of love than that for which *agapē* can account; that is, if there was an official scale to weigh the quality of love. Although *erōs* can, in theory, be described as unfailing, it cannot independently represent the fullness of God's perfect love for all people.

Philia. This form of love is associated with brotherly love and is generally experienced between parents, siblings, and close friends. If there was an official scale on which we could measure different kinds of love, *philia* would be placed on the bottom rung. Although *philia* can, in theory, be described as unfailing, it cannot independently represent the fullness of God's perfect love for all people. We can only begin to fathom the heights and depths of the inseparable threefold chord of God's unfailing love when we see each of its strands harmoniously intertwined.

Now that we have explored the triune nature of divine love, it would be tempting to assume that one of its strands is more or less significant or valuable than another—kind of like how some people understand the Trinity. The system by which I described each term almost cheapens one or more's worth, which would inevitably cheapen their collective worth—God forbid. I would like to suggest just the opposite.

What if God's love is much greater than it would have been if it was but one strand? Likewise, what if God's character, which consists of an intertwining of his attributes, is much greater than it would have been if he was but just, merciful, gracious, or loving? What if his grace, mercy, love, and justice are one in the same? What if?

Available Grace

Are you married to your understanding of postmortem judgment? Surely that sounds like a ridiculous question, but take a moment to consider its implications. We, as the Bride of Christ, are one flesh with our Groom and are committed to him till death[11] do us part.[12] Unfortunately, our perception of theological matters can affect how we understand the substance of our engagement, which can discourage us from examining what we mistakenly identify as pillars of our religion/relationship.

God's unfailing love, along with his other attributes, ought to serve as a compass as we "test all things". Since many treat nonessential doctrines as though they are essential to their faith, God's attributes are often molded around their doctrinal convictions rather than the other way around. Since ECT is widely accepted as an essential doctrine, many understand God's love, grace, mercy, and justice in light of that doctrine rather than the other way around—rather than gleaning their understanding of postmortem judgement from those attributes.

God demonstrated his love for us in that while we were *still* sinners[13] Christ died for us.[14] He did not die for his friends, but for his enemies. He loves his enemies. Therefore he died for them to make *friends* of them. He loved *us* in spite of the fact that we did not deserve it. Will such a love fail for the least of us?

If his love is *currently* unfailing for his enemies, that cannot change in the hereafter. Many rightly maintain that God's unfailing love was expressed for the entire world when Christ died for us. However, when this statement is applied to the doctrine of ECT, all sorts of problems surface. An appeal to free will was one of my favorite tactics when I defended this doctrine. I believed that since everyone has the ability to choose, no one can believe with certainty that God's love will bring the best end for all people.[15] Even though I believed that God would always love those in hell with an unfailing love, I also believed that when people crossed the threshold of death and tumbled into the retributive fires of the postmortem realm there was no longer any hope for them. I never bothered to ask *how* God's unfailing love is expressed to those in hell. [16]

Although God's unfailing love was expressed on Calvary, it was not expressed *exclusively* on Calvary. Calvary is not the unfailing love of God, but the means by which he expressed it. It was the mode by which *something*

---

11. But this will never happen because sinners will never die once they are brought back to life in Christ. Note: Everyone is spiritually dead until they are saved by grace through faith.

12. John 4:14.

13. That is, enemies of God.

14. Rom 5:8.

15. What once seemed like good news for all people turned out to be false hope for those who would inevitably die in their sins.

16. That is, enemies of God.

was offered. That something is the *actual* expression of his love because it maintains its unfailing nature. If Calvary was the actual expression of his unfailing love, the cross would lose its power over death *by* the death of those who remain in their sins.

So, what *is* the "actual expression" of God's love for the world? How was it expressed before his incarnation? How has it been expressed afterward? How *is* it expressed to the living? How *is* it expressed to the dead? Rather than trying to answer each of those questions individually, consider the following question: How is God's unfailing love expressed to those who are still in their sins?

God expressed his love for the world through Calvary. Through Jesus' death, burial, resurrection, and ascension, he made a way for sinners to be reconciled with God. Since Calvary proffers grace, we can identify grace as the means by which God expresses his love for the uncommitted. Yet what is it about grace that makes it the unfailing expression of his love? Since it is only unfailing as long as it is an expression, we can deduce that the unfailing nature of God's love depends on the *availability* of his grace.

The availability of grace, proffered through Calvary, is the ultimate expression of God's unfailing love for his enemies. Calvary *was* the means by which God offered forgiveness once and for all. It permitted grace to be the present-perfect means through which all may be reconciled. If God's love is unfailing, grace has to *remain* available for the recipients of his love. If this is true, the prevalent understanding of postmortem judgment fails because it denies the unfailing nature of God's love by placing an expiration date on his grace and mercy.

Many try to account for this discrepancy by suggesting that no one in hell will repent, even though his grace is ever-present. However, if hell's inhabitants will never come to repentance, but continuously become hardened toward his grace, then we cannot say that his grace is *actually* available. If there is no real possibility for anyone to be effected positively by grace then, technically, we cannot meaningfully say that it is available. If anyone is necessarily lost for eternity when they die, even if it is by their own "choosing", then we cannot say that God's love is unfailing for them. And *if God's love isn't unfailing for all, it isn't unfailing at all.*

When Christians appeal to the free will of the individual by suggesting that they *decide* to resist grace forever,[17] it goes something like the following: "God will always love those in hell even though they will *never* repent."

---

17. To the Calvinist: At this point, God's love has failed for those individuals, from the foundation of the world. God deliberately chose not to "lift the veil" from their eyes. So, grace was never truly available to those who never really had a chance to respond to it.

Many fail to realize that love is much more than a fluttering of butterflies in one's tummy. Authentic love *requires* an actual expression of that love, much like authentic faith requires actual fruit to verify its authenticity.

Some believe that God expresses his love for those who die in their sins by giving them what they want—absolutely nothing to do with him.[18] Is this really the case? Do the unrepentant want nothing to do with God? Would it be loving to allow our loved ones to do harm to themselves, especially if the consequences are irrevocable? Moreover, is leaving the uncommitted in a state of unbearable misery, which encourages them to want nothing to do with God, really giving them what they want? If so, this hypothetical effect of postmortem judgment[19] ultimately falls on the shoulders of he who created the predicament more than it does on anyone else.[20] And if those who are damned to hell are unable to come to repentance, then God's grace is not actually available, his love is not unfailing, and death trumps the cross.

---

18. Ironically, postmortem judgment has everything to do with him.
19. That is, perpetual rebellion.
20. This is no less true if the doctrine of conditional immortality prevails.

6

Unscrupulous Justice

> There is a difference between what is wrong and what is evil. Evil is committed when clarity is taken away from what is clearly wrong, allowing wrong to be seen as less wrong, excusable, right, or an obligatory commandment of the Lord God Almighty. . . . Evil is bad sold as good, wrong sold as right, injustice sold as justice. Like the coat of a virus, a thin veil of right can disguise enormous wrong and confer an ability to infect others.
>
> —JOHN HARTUNG

WHEN PEOPLE READ OR hear statements, like Hartung's, that implicitly challenge their theological or philosophical convictions, their natural reaction is to tune them out or to ignore them altogether. I can recall many occasions when I did just that. As far as I was concerned, those who disagreed with my beliefs about postmortem judgement had little to no credibility when it came to spiritual matters.

When Christians face scrutiny, one of our first objectives is to identify the worldview of our interrogator. For instance, when conspiracy theorists opine on events like the 9/11 terrorist attack in New York City or the Apollo 11's moon landing, they are rarely taken seriously. Similarly, when Christians come to realize that they are being cross-examined by an unbeliever, they usually feel obliged to dismiss their claims because, as far as many are concerned, unbelievers are nothing more than glorified conspiracy theorists when it comes to spirituality.

Just as most people disregard conspiracy theories like the New World Order or population control, most Christians tend to disregard an atheist's concerns regarding theology.[1] As Christians, we should not dismiss any-

---

1. Christians are occasionally treated similarly if they disagree with established

one's concerns simply because we disagree with them because that reaction could be detrimental to our evangelical and spiritual maturation, which, in turn, may have a counterproductive effect on someone's journey to Christ or spiritual maturation.

When orthodoxy is hit with an onslaught of probing questions, cognitive dissonance quickly takes effect—which encourages Christians to act passive-aggressively or to, at best, disregard someone's concerns. I have participated in and witnessed discussions between skeptics and believers of every stripe. Along the way, I have discovered that there are far more *agnostics* than there are anti-theists actively investigating the Christian Faith. Therefore, we can safely conclude that most of the scrutiny that Christians receive from unbelievers comes from those who are not necessarily anti-God.

Even when Christians are scrutinized by anti-theists, we do not have any more leverage in disregarding their *concerns* than we do with anyone else. However, at the end of the day, lost is still lost; spiritual deadness is still spiritual deadness; a spiritual handicap is still a spiritual handicap. It is not until our Creator resurrects our spirits and heals our spiritual disabilities that we become alive to spiritual truths—or so we have been told.

A great many Christians believe that unbelievers are unable to fathom spiritual truths because they are legally blind—they cannot see what they cannot fathom. Just as someone who has been blind since birth cannot comprehend the meaning of light or its luminance, neither can those who are spiritually blind fathom spiritual colors or their hues.

My Calvinistic *familia*-in-Christ is likely thrilled to have finally read something sensible. On the other hand, the last couple paragraphs are probably frustrating for my Arminian siblings. As a *former* Arminian who considered Calvinistic theology, I can see how many Christians find its premises appealing, maybe even convicting, because I nearly adopted its systematic theology on at least one occasion. Even though it did not survive my theological interrogations, I was never fully satisfied with its counterpart either—Arminianism. One side seemed to minimize our responsibility and the other side seemed to minimize God's. Although neither fully answered my questions without leaving me with many more, I saw Arminianism as less damaging to God's character and image.

As a Christian Universalist, I now reject both paradigms. Just as Christians who accept the doctrine of annihilation or ECT follow Arminian or Augustinian[2] theology, some Christians who accept the doctrine of Universal Reconciliation have attempted to incorporate Arminian or Augustinian orthodoxy.

---

2. Calvinism.

theological presuppositions into their paradigm. Even though the doctrine of Conditional Immortality allows its adherents to be Calvinists or Arminians, the doctrine of Universal Reconciliation does not.

In *The Evangelical Universalist*, Gregory MacDonald[3] explores how Calvinism and Arminianism effect their perception of God's omnipotence and omnibenevolence. He demonstrates each's perspective of God's will and demonstrates how each paradigm determines the manner in which God ultimately "gets what he wants." Both paradigms are allegedly built on a foundation that is good and just. Yet just as is the case with every human-made doctrine, which includes CU, their foundation is built on an *interpretation* of Scripture rather than on unquestionable truths. ECT and CI presuppose that the gospel is no longer effective after death, which affects their perception of God's attributes. CU rejects that presupposition and is, thereby, freed from having to wrestle with God's attributes.

Calvinism depends on the validity of several presuppositions. It focuses primarily on God's omnipotence. Yet in the process, it minimizes his omnibenevolence—the measure of his love—by asserting that, although God loves everyone, he does not love everyone *equally*. It maintains that he has a "special" love for the Elect in an attempt to justify his apparent passivity regarding the salvation of many. Since it presupposes that the gospel is no longer effective after death and due to the fact that many die before they respond positively to the gospel, it proclaims that God does not desire to save everyone. Otherwise, he *would* bring everyone to repentance *before* they die. Wherein sin abounds, grace abounds—a little bit.[4]

Arminianism also depends on the validity of several presuppositions. It focuses primarily on God's omnibenevolence. Yet in the process, it minimizes his omnipotence—the measure of his sovereignty—by asserting that, although God desires to save everyone, he cannot violate anyone's freewill. Since it presupposes that the gospel is no longer effective after death and due to the fact that many die before they respond positively to the gospel, it proclaims that God *cannot* accomplish his will in its fullness. Otherwise, he *would* bring everyone to repentance *before* they die. Wherein sin abounds, grace abounds—a little bit.

Christian Universalism also depends on the validity of several presuppositions. However, it does not focus primarily on one of God's attributes over any other. Therefore, its presuppositions are not as problematic. Some believe that it creates issue with God's justice, but I would like to suggest

---

3. a pseudonym of Robin A. Parry
4. This is a paraphrase of a statement made by Robin Parry.

otherwise. CU produces questions about *one* of God's attributes[5] while the other two paradigms produce questions and causes strife between all of them. CU does not minimize God's omnibenevolence—the measure of his love—because it affirms that he loves everyone *equally*. Neither does it minimize God's omnipotence—his ability to accomplish his will—because it *rejects* the presupposition that the gospel is no longer effective after death. Since it presupposes that grace is always available[6]—that death does not restrain the gospel—even for those who die before they respond positively to the gospel, it proclaims that God desires to save everyone and that he is able to do so—that everyone will ultimately drink from the well of living water and never thirst again.[7] According to this paradigm, God does not handicap humankind by enforcing counterproductive restrictions on the road to their eternal destiny. Wherein sin abounds, grace abounds—much, much more.

With these three paradigms in mind, how does the popular understanding of "spiritual deadness" relate? Are unbelievers necessarily ignorant of spiritual matters? Is that even possible? I believe the answers to those questions depend on whether or not the uncommitted can be held responsible for a lifetime of spiritual rebellion. Conveniently, the Bible has something to say about that. It explicitly states that *no one* will have an excuse for dying in their sins.[8] Although it is easy for us to see *that* this is taught in the Bible, can we see why this is true?

Creation's Proclamation

One of the Bible's most emphatic messages is that the universe screams the name of its Maker. C. S. Lewis once stated, "I felt in my bones that this universe does not explain itself." According to the First Cause argument, any finite existent must have an external source. It also asserts that the only existent that does not require an external source is the *original* source, the source of all sources—the necessarily transcendent First Cause/Principle.

Since the universe, according to science, *began* to exist, it requires an external source and is, therefore, not transcendent—since the transcendent transcends space-time and can, therefore, not *begin* to exist. Any particular existent that *began* to exist can be traced back to its source, which can, if it began to exist, be traced back to the necessarily self-existent First Cause.

---

5. That is, justice.

6. Chapter 5 explains how grace must remain available if divine love is to maintain any semblance to a love that is truly unfailing.

7. John 4:14; 7:38.

8. Rom 1:20.

Likewise, spiritual truths—if there is any objectivity to spiritual claims—are dependent on their first principle, which scripture identifies as God's "invisible attributes."[9]

Contrary to the opinion of many Christians, if the uncommitted can be held responsible for dying in their sins, they *must* also have the ability to determine the viability of spiritual claims; particularly, that they are in need of salvation. It does not logically follow that the uncommitted are unable to determine the truthfulness of spiritual claims simply because they lack faith in Christ. Otherwise, salvation would be an impossibility and the repercussions for a lack of faith would be arbitrary. The Gospel presupposes the uncommitted are able to determine the viability of the spiritual claim that they are lost and in need of a Savior. If humankind can perceive God's eternal power and divine nature through what he had made, they are thereby capable of perceiving spiritual truths, which, consequently, leaves them without excuse on the Day of Judgment.[10]

Sincere Apprehension

As a Christian, have you ever considered the possibility that unbelievers may not be looking for reasons to disbelieve?[11] At times, many appear to be doing just that, but what if their questions stem from issues that genuinely concern them? What if the facade of the new atheism camouflages issues that should concern us? The more I think about all of this, the more I am convinced that many of their concerns are genuine roadblocks for them, none of which they can simply ignore. When Christians disregard the concerns of unbelievers, they stray from being beacons that are designed to illuminate the path for the wayward and become dimmed obstacles that trip-up the lost sheep of his pasture.[12]

---

9. If there is an absolute sense of right and wrong, one must ask, "By what standard can we measure such objectivity?" If genocide is immoral, as proponents to classical theism claim, there must be an authoritative source from which such laws find their objectivity. The whims of human opinion do not suffice.

10. It is important to note that many who reject the Christian claims about Christ do so not solely because they reject some spiritual truth, such as the need for repentance, but also because they assess the historical evidence differently; just as Christians assess the historical evidence about the prophet Mohammed differently than do adherents to Islam.

11. Apologetics is not about proving the existence of God, but about breaking through one's will to disbelieve.

12. Ps 100:1–3.

Allegedly, most unbelievers reject Christ because of the stigma that ECT has placed on the Christian faith. They may possess a long list of reasons for their skepticism, but most of the items on that list have to do with what is perceived as injustice on God's part. In their eyes, the prevalent stance on postmortem judgment does not line up with a god that is worthy of worship. Are they, and many Christians, correct with this assessment? Even if they are, most Christians do not see this doctrine as a legitimate obstacle because they, for one reason or another, are either unaware of its inconsistencies or they chalk them up to unreliable "human reasoning."

Like Pascal, many Christians believe that persistent disbelief is nonsensical. Yet from an unbeliever's perspective, the gospel is not *believable* as long as it is riddled with inconsistencies. Although we can argue that those who have not tasted the sweetness of God's salvific grace do not understand what biblical faith is all about, they may be in a better place to pinpoint inconsistencies that are hidden among prevalent theological presuppositions.

Since every single Christian rejects at least one doctrine that another Christian accepts, how can we dismiss similar concerns when they come from unbelievers? For every Christian that rejects a doctrine that another Christian accepts, there is at least one unbeliever who has similar concerns.

How do *you* feel about the idea that your husband or wife, mother or father, son or daughter, friend or foe could end up in hell—hopelessly trapped in a place, or state of being, that purposefully inflicts the most agonizing pain imaginable without a single opportunity for grace or repentance, for no good purpose beyond "retribution"? On the other hand, how do you feel about the idea that your husband or wife, mother or father, son or daughter, friend or foe could end up in hell—*purposely* confined in a place, or state of being, that is for their better good?[13]

Which option is more worthy of God? Given what we know about him, can we expect one over the other? The typical reaction toward this is: "Who are you, O man, to question God? Is he not the Potter? Are you not the clay? Can the clay say to the Potter—why have you formed me thus?" Although this reaction is motivated by Scripture, we must question whether or not its general application is the result of exegesis or cognitive dissonance.

---

13. Hell must have been created before the end of day seven—the completion of creation. At the end of the seventh day, God declared all things "very good." Therefore, hell was declared "good", even if it may not appear that way for those experiencing it—similar to how our children do not feel like the consequences for their actions are for their own good.

Who Can Resist His Will?

So then he has mercy on whomever he wills, and he hardens whomever he wills.

You will say to me then, "Why does he still find fault? Who can resist his will?"

But who are you, O man, to answer back to God? Will what is molded say to its molder,

"Why have you made me like this?" Has the potter no right over the clay, to make out of the same lump one vessel for honorable use and another for dishonorable use?

—ROMANS 9:18–21

Regardless of how forcibly many Christians insist that Christianity is not a religion that requires them to "check their brains in at the door", many will not hesitate to disregard anything that challenges orthodoxy. Although authoritative figures in the church encourage Christians to have an answer ready for anyone who asks about their faith, a swift and decisive, "Who are you, O man, to question your Potter?" is usually the default response when anyone questions the doctrine of ECT.[14] As a Christian who was conditioned to conform to orthodoxy and sheltered from differing points of view, I understand the genuine intent and motivation behind this knee-jerk reaction. I was lead to believe that rebuke was the biblical response to "unhealthy" skepticism.

According to orthodoxy: The Bible is true whether we like it or not. If God says something, who are we to say otherwise? If he has determined that something is just, how in the world could we beg to differ? He *is* the Potter. We are but clay—the dust of the earth. What can we add or take away from anything that he has spoken?

Even though I no longer accept the doctrine of ECT, I agree with the implications behind each of those questions/statements. We are merely a speck, apart from Christ, in a vast cosmos that was created by he who is far more complex, yet simplistic,[15] than we can imagine. The absurd idea of the created even beginning to form a legitimate contention against what

---

14. Seeing how many react so unapologetically toward their own family in Christ, the uncommitted are not usually caught off guard when they are treated similarly by professing Christians.

15. A. W. Tozer's *The Knowledge of the Holy* does an amazing job explaining the mind-boggling complexity and simplicity of God.

its Creator has determined evidences the magnitude of our dire need for redemption and restoration. The mortal are in absolutely no condition to critique the immortal. If God has determined that certain repercussions for defiance are just, we could never meaningfully suggest otherwise. Any intention to add or take away a single jot or tittle from what he has decreed would be in vain and would attest to just how inept we are as we grasp for the hem of his celestial garments.[16]

In his epistle to the Romans, Paul addressed a point of contention similar to one that is often raised by skeptics today. Paul acknowledged that they were correct in believing that no one can resist the sovereign will of God,[17] yet their argument was the byproduct of unspoken presuppositions. They jumped from a single verbal premise to a conclusion and, therefore, came to an illogical and unscriptural conclusion regarding the responsibility of the uncommitted. Given that no one can resist the sovereign will of God, they inquired, "Why does he still find fault?"

Many believe that this passage demonstrates why we should not challenge God. That idea may have layered truths to it, but it is not an accurate portrayal of the point Paul was trying to make. It is important to realize that those who challenge the justness of ECT are not necessarily questioning God, but a theological proposition—a proposition that does not encourage a healthy reverence[18] toward God, but an unholy trepidation toward him. The implications of this doctrine are far more adverse than is the Good News that Christ brought for *all people*.

Even though we live in an advanced technological era, we are no less prone to error than anyone throughout the history of the world. Humanity has not changed much in the last two-thousand years. We still desire the same things, struggle with the same problems, long for the same reliefs, and stumble into the same pits. Likewise, ever since the time of Christ, people have rejected the gospel for essentially the same reasons.

With a similar intent, Paul's audience asked the same questions we ask today, albeit in different words. Much like today, the uncommitted attempted to find a detour around the direct route to reconciliation with God. They inquired, in so many words, "Are we not good enough to gain favor with our Maker? Since God can do as he pleases, can he not show grace apart from Christ? Can he not choose to look over times of disobedience as he 'looked

---

16. Even though I agree with prevalent presuppositions in this regard, somethings (or someone?) is drawing me away from certain implications.

17. 2 Chr 20:6; Job 9:12; Dan 4:35.

18. Isa 29:13.

over times of ignorance,' rather than 'command all people everywhere to repent'?[19] Why does he still find fault!?"

By asking that final question, they were asking something a bit deeper than what you or I may notice at first glance. Several verses earlier, Paul mentioned God's inherent *right* to show mercy or wrath on those of his choosing. If we were to take those verses by themselves, his choosing would seem arbitrary. Some people use this passage as a proof-text for their understanding of predestination. However, if we interpret those verses in context and apply it to the passage that asks, "Why does he still find fault?", the predestinarian's soteriology would conflict with the theme of Paul's epistle.

With whom is God merciful? Who is the recipient of his wrath? "He is merciful to and wrathful toward those of his choosing." seems to be a fitting reply, but that does not fully answer the question. God desires/wills to have mercy on *everyone*, but he is obligated, by his holy nature, to inflict wrath on some.[20] In light of the fact that he desires to have mercy on everyone, which includes the recipients of his wrath, we should ask, "What is the *purpose* of his wrath?" Scriptures states that "vengeance is mine, sayeth the Lord." What does that look like? Does it look similar to ours? How is it different?

Since we know that God's desire is for no one to perish,[21] but for all to come to repentance,[22] it follows that he does not desire to express wrath on anyone for its own sake. Since he desires to have mercy on all, could it be that he desires to express wrath on the unrepentant, in order to bring them to repentance, *so that* he can justly have mercy on all? Could it be that he desires to bring everyone into the *category* which has been predestined to be shown mercy and conformed into the image of his Son?[23] If so, we could say that God kills *to* make alive; he destroys *to make way* for restoration; he brings us down/humbles us in order to lift us up.

By asking, "Why does he still find fault?", they were asking essentially the same question unbelievers ask today—"Why can't he have mercy on both the repentant and unrepentant?" That question, which blasphemes the purpose of Christ, rightfully invited Paul's rebuke, "Who are you, O man, to answer back to God?"

As one of the first Christian apologists, Paul addressed their reaction before it had time to form. He was not rebuking them for misunderstanding

---

19. Acts 17:30.

20. His obligation to inflict wrath on some does not prevent him from eventually showering mercy on all, once Christ meets the prerequisites in them.

21. That is, to suffer from his wrath.

22. 2 Pet 3:9.

23. Rom 8:29.

postmortem judgment or any other nonessential doctrine. Rather, he rebuked them for challenging something essential to the Christian Faith: the need for a repentant heart, which produces its natural fruit—a committed life to Christ, to Love incarnate.

**

Have you ever wondered why many say, "The grass is always greener on the other side of the fence."? What is it about "that" that makes it more appealing than "this"? In this analogy, grass has many possible applications. However, there are other useful details that are often overlooked. The dullness of the grass on "this" side of the fence represents discontentment with what is familiar and, therefore, naturally directs our attention toward its counterpart—the unfamiliar "over there". Discontentment leads to covetousness, and covetousness distracts from the underlying problem that is responsible for a discontented life.

Imagine a pasture within the enclosure of a white picket fence. Each board that makes up the exterior fencing represents the general, yet essential,[24] concept of postmortem judgment. As Christians, those who are within acknowledge that it is a necessary component of their biblical worldview. As you glance across the enclosure, you notice a fifth section of fencing that divides the enclosure into two separate compartments.

Those within the larger section of the enclosure fail to see much of a difference between the dividing section of the fencing and the exterior sides. Most of them see the fifth/dividing section as though it is the forth. Therefore, they tend to blend Christians in the second section with unbelievers outside of the Christian fold. In the meantime, those who are actually on the outside looking in can only see the exterior, which differentiates the committed from the uncommitted. Since the prevalent view prevails within the fold, those from without understand the finer details of the perimeter according to the prevalent description from those within. If the majority of those who are within are never told that there is more than one Christian view of postmortem judgement, or if they refuse to consider that possibility, those who are without will likely jump on the bandwagon as they are gradually won over to the Faith or as they argue against the Christian religion.

For some reason, Christians are taught to use the doctrine of ECT as an evangelical tool in a manner similar to Pascal's Wager. Although it may be somewhat successful with unbelievers who do not have logical reasons

---

24. If there were no judgment, there would be no need for Jesus. Therefore, postmortem judgment is necessary for there to be a need for a Savior.

for their lack of faith, it is often counterproductive with intellectuals. Moreover, if the uncommitted use the prevalent doctrine of postmortem judgement as a crutch for their lack of faith—as their "excuse" in the sea of excuselessness—we can decide to take their concerns seriously and test them *or* we can continue to ignore them and presume that their insight is of no value when it comes to theology, which requires us to assume that Christians who sympathize with their concerns are either deceived or intentionally dishonest.

Many believers *and* unbelievers are convinced that the prevalent doctrine of postmortem judgment is an enormous wrong that has been disguised with a thin veil of light; namely, the presupposition that ECT is the will of God and is, therefore, good and true. Is the endless conscious torment of those who die in their sins good and true? Or is it seen as good and true because it has been *deemed* the will of God?

Consider George MacDonald's opinion on this matter: "If a man see in God any darkness at all, and especially if he defend that darkness, attempting to justify it as one who respects the person of God, I cannot but think his blindness must have followed his mockery of 'Lord! Lord!' Surely, if he had been strenuously obeying Jesus, he would ere now have received the truth that God is light, and in him is no darkness—a truth which is not acknowledged by calling the darkness attributed to him light, and the candle of the Lord in the soul of man darkness. It is one thing to believe that God can do nothing wrong, quite another to call whatever presumption we may attribute to him right."[25]

Since God instructs Christians to destroy evil with good,[26] I cannot help but suspect that he intends to do the same.

---

25. George MacDonald, "The Truth in Jesus," in *Unspoken Sermons: Series i, ii, and iii*. 2012. Kindle edition. First published 1867–89.

26. Rom 12:2.

7

Grace, Mercy, and Love vs Justice

> Great is the guilt of an unnecessary war.
> —JOHN ADAMS

WHEN WE HEAR OF wars, or rumors of wars, many picture bullets whizzing by the heads of women and small children. Some visualize the unnecessary destruction of thousands upon thousands of *human beings* who willingly give up their lives for the "freedoms" of others. Many sympathize with those who happened to be on the "wrong side" of the "fight." Yet there are some, perhaps many, who maintain that war is a necessary evil that the world *must* endure for the greater good of us all.

Even though we usually call to mind gruesome images at the mention of this term, "war" is also an accurate description of everyday circumstances, even if they are not as extreme. Although the tangible loss and pain is of a different type, the strife between different systems of philosophical and theological ideologies has had much more of an effect on civilization than many could have predicted. Church history is littered with cases upon cases of events that testify to just how far people are willing to go to preserve their dogmas. Christian martyrs, who have been labeled as enemies of the church, have died at the hands of professing Christians no less than they have died at the hands of those who were openly antichrist.

Rather than allowing iron to sharpen iron,[1] the weak profess to be warriors. They beat their plowshares into swords and their pruning hooks into spears as they invade neighboring communities and declare war against their allies—essentially shattering the very hones on which they should be sharpening their swords and burning down the arenas in which they should

---

1. Prov 27:17.

be sparring with their allies. The Augustinian–Arminian schism is a prime example of such an atrocity.

To conclude Section 2, I would like to focus on the predominant dilemma within the doctrine of ECT. In the previous three chapters, we examined how this doctrine effects our perception of God's attributes; that is, if we believe that it is valid. If it is true, then we have to accept that God's love is deficient for most people, that his grace and mercy is in a state of decay, and that his justice is apparently unscrupulous.

If, as I have suggested, the plausibility of ECT depends on a skewed perception of God's attributes, we should be able to determine which misconception of the three listed in the previous three chapters is primarily responsible for the formation of this doctrine. Since few who follow Jesus openly accept those descriptions of God's attributes, their acceptance of ECT seemingly cannot be traced back to a single presupposition about any of God's attributes. However, I doubt that a misconception of the entire lot is to blame.

When ECT is openly scrutinized, its conception of justice usually draws more scrutiny than its conception of his other attributes. When someone defends the doctrine, they do not claim that it is true because God is gracious, merciful, or loving. They say that it is true because God is *just*. They claim that it is just because God is just. However, few claim that it is loving, merciful, and gracious because God is loving, merciful, and gracious. They spend enough time trying to make sense out of it justness to consider other requisites.

Fear—Taught by the Commandment of Men

> These people draw near with their mouths and honor me with their lips, but have removed their hearts far from me, and their fear toward me is taught by the commandment of men.

Why do so many Christians believe that the disease of our hearts can only be treated in this present age? Many appeal to supposed proof-texts for this belief, but few have a defense for their understanding of these texts. As I have stated previously, few seem to understand why they believe as they do. One of the problems with presuppositions, in general, is that many tend to see them as points of faith rather than as things that deserve to be tested as much as any other philosophical or theological proposition.

Is there a sound defense for the claim that salvation is only available before we die? If so, what is it about the death of our bodies that prevents the consequences of sin from having their natural reformative effect on us hereafter? If there is an answer to these questions, the Bible has little to say about it, one way or the other.

The Bible states that once a New Covenant arrives, the Old Covenant passes away. It also states that those who do not believe are condemned *already*. Scripture also seems to suggest that those who are not in Christ will be judged under the Old Covenant, which explains why they are *already* condemned.[2] In contrast, those who believe in him are condemned *no longer*, which implies that they were *once* condemned via disbelief. The following verse explains why the uncommitted are condemned, in a present-perfect sense: "Although God overlooked the times of ignorance, now he commands all people everywhere to repent."

As Christians, we are no longer under the Law/Old Covenant, but under grace.[3] Therefore, the uncommitted are no longer condemned merely for failing to live up to the standard of Old Testament Law, but for failing to abide by a *single* law—to believe in the name of the only Son of God.[4] In other words, the lost have not been "found" because they have not decided to return.

If grace, at any point in the future, were to become unavailable, the uncommitted would no longer be guilty for that which substantiates their condemnation. Can anyone be guilty for rejecting Christ when accepting him is no longer an effective option? If there is no invitation for the prodigal to return, can God blame them for not returning? If God decided to remove any opportunity for the unrepentant to repent, he could not justly condemn them for remaining unrepentant;[5] that is, unless he "sanctifies" an unjust act by performing the injustice.

If mainstream Christianity would acknowledge that the perpetual availability of grace is a fundamental aspect of justice, they could not deny the possibility of postmortem reconciliation.[6] Thereafter, the church would have to amend the orthodox depiction of postmortem judgment, which would initiate a widespread assurance in God's unfailing love, perpetual

---

2. Rom 8:13.
3. Rom 6:14; Gal 3:23–26.
4. Acts 17:30.
5. Calvinism fails for similar reasons.
6. As long as something is "available," there must be a possibility for someone to accept it. Otherwise, it is not "actually" available.

grace and mercy, and victorious justice—which would, in turn, foreshadow an assurance in the ultimate reconciliation of all things.[7]

***

For as long as anyone can remember, evangelicals have used the concept of ECT as a means to an end. It has been preached from the pulpit as a means to motivate/coerce the lost to say "the sinner's prayer" or to motivate/coerce Christians to "rededicate" their lives to Jesus. Some evangelicals even spend their days over the deathbeds of the terminally ill with pamphlets that vividly describe what they are in for if they die outside of God's good favor—as though the created has to gain the favor of its Creator. Unfortunately, this mindset has caused many to believe that the gospel basically says, "You have until the end of your life to love me."[8]

Although this tactic has been somewhat successful in each of the scenarios listed above, its effectiveness has been declining rapidly as of late. Some Christians attribute this to a lack of fervor, while others attribute it to end-time prophecy. Rather than assuming this or that, the fact that the New Testament has no trace of this tactic being used during Jesus' ministry or immediately afterward should have drawn our attention long before now. There is good reason to believe that Jesus did not authorize this tactic, not only for reasons stated above, but also because it does not have a foundation in early church practices.[9]

According to ancient archives,[10] Christian Universalism was the prevalent doctrine of postmortem judgement during the first five/hundred years of church history. Even though it is easy to emphasize the most favorable point if view when giving a case for my view, I will work with the idea that each doctrine of postmortem judgment had somewhat of a balanced following during its adolescent years.[11]

In defense of ECT, many mistakenly assume that God would not allow his church to be in error for so long without correction. Is this a valid presupposition? When has God ever miraculously corrected false doctrine

---

7. Section 3 will substantiate this claim.

8. This is a strange mindset not only because it violates the essence of authentic love, but also because he who desires our love also determines the length of our lives.

9. That is, during its infancy.

10. See John Wesley Hanson's *Universalism: The Prevailing Doctrine of the Christian Church during Its First Five Hundred Years*, listed in Appendix D.

11. This, of course, ignores the fact that there were more second-century schools that taught UR than there were that taught ECT or CU; 4:1:1, to be exact. See Appendix C.

on a wide scale? The Apostle Paul could be considered as a single example of such a thing, but he is one case out of billions. According to Scripture, Israel rejected every prophet that God had sent her. They never had a Damascus-like experience. Neither did God do away with the Jewish sacrificial system (AD 70) for about thirty-seven years after Jesus fulfilled the Old Covenant (AD 33).

If we know anything about church history, or even the present day, we should be well aware of the many dishonorable, if not outright evil, acts that have been committed in the name of God. Even if someone is not savvy with history or modern-day events, they should be well aware that God has not limited the amount of time he will allow Christians to believe incorrectly or to live ungodly lives. Many fail to realize that God *permits* us to follow the desires of our hearts because he wants *us* to choose *him*, as he chose us.[12]

Everything that God wants us to know about him is discoverable. It is readily available through both special and natural revelation—scripture and nature—and has likely been accepted by someone somewhere, yet understood by no one in its entirety. In this present darkness, the possibility of reaching theological perfection is no more likely than the possibility of reaching sinless perfection prior to the day when Jesus will have made all things new.

Technically, theological perfection requires an omniscient source, which is the exclusive identity of deity,[13] and an omniscient interpreter, which is the identity of no human on earth. Therefore, we should be humbled by our obvious inferiority and tendency to err as we strive to understand nonessential doctrines of the Christian faith. Since every Christian believes that their theological conviction are correct, many refuse to acknowledge that all nonessential theological systems have been systematized by *fallible* human beings. Even if the Bible is inerrant, which I do not deny, it does not lay out a single systematic theological system beyond that which is essential to the Faith.

God expects us to explore and test theological propositions, regardless of whether or not they are essential to saving faith. If Christians, for one reason or another, become complacent in their theological walk, if we cease to test all things,[14] our relationship with God will suffer along the way. In we desire to maintain a healthy relationship with our Creator, we must

---

12. He has chosen us by dying for us, but we must choose him like any bride "chooses" her groom by accepting his proposal.

13. Technically, God does not need to *interpret* anything since he is omniscient.

14. 1 Thess 5:21.

become theologically proactive because theological passivity is detrimental to spiritual vitality.

The Son of God was very solemn about the sincerity of those who *claimed* to be servants of his Father. He never attempted to conceal his disdain for those who pretended like they were all in. He never spoke in parables regarding this aspect of the Faith, but plainly stated that we should be either hot or cold—he will spew the *lukewarm* out of his mouth.[15] In other words, Jesus was much more tolerant of those who were anti-Christ than he was of those who *took his name*[16] in vain.

There is no such thing as neutral territory or middle ground in the life of a Christian. Moreover, stillness in our walk with God is a contradiction in terms, unless it pertains to taking a moment to "be still and know that [he is] God."[17] We are either maturing in our spirituality or we are not Jesus' disciples. On the Day of Judgment, many will claim to have performed mighty works in his name, but they will be in for a rude awakening when they realize that he never knew them, nor they him.[18]

***

It has become customary for authoritative figures in the church to discourage *their* sheep from exploring unfamiliar terrain. I have witnessed several cases in which congregations were discouraged from reading a book or an article because it challenged the prevalent presuppositions of their particular denomination. At times, such dissuasions are so subtle that many fail to realize what they are hearing. Others do not bother with subtleties.

I once heard a pastor say to his congregation, with book in hand, "Have any of you read *this* book? No?. . . then don't!" Shortly thereafter, he brashly compared CU to actual cults.[19] The cults with which he grouped CU were labeled correctly as cultic; not necessarily because of their understanding of nonessential doctrines, but more so because of their rejection of what *is* essential to the Christian faith—that Jesus died, his resurrection, humanity, sinlessness, and so forth.

---

15. Rev 3:15–16.
16. Taking someone's name is an idiom for marriage.
17. Ps 46:10.
18. Matt 7:21–23.
19. Thus using an *ad hominem* argument.

Steve Gregg[20] once described a cult more or less as a religious gathering that is forbidden to question what their organization has stamped as "correct theology". He went on to explain how certain denominations have similar cult-like tendencies. Even though they may not forbid their congregants from investigating prominent dogmas, many are strongly discourage from doing so. Although many church gatherings possess this cult-like similarity, most of them do not actually leap over the cultic barbed wire fencing into anathematized pastures.[21]

Christian Universalists accept and teach essential doctrines that the likes of Jehovah's Witnesses and Mormons do not. On the same token, unlike those cults and unlike many orthodox churches, CU does not discourage anyone from questioning its claims. Since many do not understand how an evangelical can reject ECT, many believe that an evangelical Christian Universalist is a misnomer.

Before many even attempt to look into alternate theological possibilities, they have already determined their stance on the matter. I appreciate how difficult it is to understand how a Christian can believe in Universal Reconciliation[22] without cheapening the work of the cross[23] because I once struggled with the idea. I once thought that those who believe in UR must deny some essential truth of the Christian faith or fail to uphold the authority of Scripture. I eventually discovered that I was the one who failed to realize how my understanding of justice unharmonized the trifecta of God's grace/mercy, love, and justice. Thereafter, I decided to set all of my preconceived notions aside[24] and to read the Bible with a heart to determine whether or not ECT was as dense throughout its pages as I had always assumed.

There is not a single day that goes by when I fail to hear someone on the radio or in church claim that something is true with little more than a hearty, "Thus sayeth the Lord." You may have realized this already, but one of my biggest pet peeves is when Christians say something is true "just because it is" or simply because "the Bible says so." Even though it may seem to imply otherwise, that does not disqualify me from being an evangelical.

Due to my natural tendency to be a bit overconfident in what I have accepted as truth, I have made intentional efforts to limit its effect on my

---

20. Steve Gregg is an author, radio host, and owner of www.thenarrowpath.com.
21. Unfortunately, they do not often return the grace that is shown toward them.
22. Col 1:19, 20.
23. Section 3 will explore this concept.
24. This is not to say that I or anyone else ever thinks that we have not already set those notions aside.

approach to new data; primarily because absolute certainty about nonessential issues could discourage me from sincerely considering alternate doctrinal possibilities. It is natural to assume that our theological convictions are more obvious than they actually are, which can cause us to think negatively about those who believe differently. Yet if the Bible is as explicit regarding nonessential doctrines as many presuppose, why do Christian's disagree about such a variety of issues?

Many Christians, who accept ECT, have acknowledged that salvation is not primarily about avoiding hell. Some have even suggested that those who became believe in Christ just to avoid hell should question whether or not they are actually saved. Is it possible to believe in ECT without using the doctrine as an evangelical tool? I suppose, but have rarely seen it work out that way. Since the gospel is God-centered, our presentation of it ought to to be God-centered. Yet when the uncommitted are compelled to repent so that they can avoid ECT, the theme of the Bible is turned on its head; the center of attention is redirected from God to us.

Although it is wise to obtain fire insurance and to recommend that others do likewise, if a person is "saved, but only as through fire,"[25] we might want to think twice about painting such a horrid picture of eschatological flames. Rather than directing the lost into the arms of him whom the Bible describes as a Consuming Fire,[26] we may be chasing his prodigal children in the opposite direction—right into the frigid recesses of Outer Darkness.[27] Judgement *is* coming and it *should* be feared, but we should not ignore how God's attributes should effect our understanding of his judgements. Justice *is* due, but so is grace, mercy, and love.

***

During a particular Sunday morning service—after the pastor had concluded his message and after the music director strummed his final chord—the youth pastor was closing the service with some final thoughts. Seeing how I, at the time, attended a Southern Baptist church that taught the prevalent doctrine of hell, I should have been the last person caught off guard by the situation in which I had placed myself.

Following his closing words, I hit a new low. I thought to myself, "Why should I even bother? What effect can I expect to make; not only among the

---

25. 1 Cor 3:15.
26. Deut 4:24; Heb 12:29.
27. Matt 25:30.

church as a whole, but even among this small congregation? It's not like this doctrine is up for discussion." Right before the clock struck noon, the walls came crashing down. Just before the youth pastor closed the service, he gave thanks to God for our pastor who, according to him, was "bold enough to not just skip over what is ignored by so many churches." I pondered, "Why does he assume that it takes intestinal fortitude to 'preach to the choir'?"

Since I was recently in their shoes, I understood their perspective. Church congregants are conditioned to interpret conflict as though it is their cross to bear and are commissioned to stand firm in their convictions, regardless of whether or not they pertain to essential doctrines.[28] Regardless of what type of a person decides to critique alleged inconsistencies in orthodoxy—whether it is an atheist, someone of a different religion, or a "liberal" Christian—they are usually seen as though they are just one in a multitude of skeptics who oppose other essential Christian doctrines.

In the eyes of many, Christian Universalists are blended in with the "hostile masses" that Jesus predicted would persecute his followers or lead them into false teachings. Jesus forewarned his disciples that they would be persecuted so they could prepare themselves for martyrdom—which they did. However, since his warning is applicable beyond its immediate context, many have interpreted whatever mode of conflict they happen to be in as a fulfillment of his prediction, which reinforces their presuppositions.

Unfortunately, Jesus' words are not resistant to misapplications. Due to a overly-literalistic hermeneutic, many of Jesus' followers misapply this admonition to circumstances that have nothing to do with martyrdom or persecution. Consequently, nonessential doctrines, like ECT, are treated as though they are essential the Christian Faith. Since many believe that their supposed persecution is the result of their loyalty to the biblical worldview and the authority of Scripture, many interpret contention as an affirmation of their presuppositions, which justifies their dismissive attitudes toward alternate theological possibilities.[29]

***

I rarely took statements like the youth pastor's personally. It would have been naïve of me to allow statements that coincide with a church's constitution to offend me because I knew what I was signing up for when I joined the church. What bothered me the most was not simply what came out of

---

28. Many Christians have come to expect unbelievers and even professing Christians with a "liberal" bend to disagree with their "God-given" views.

29. Keep in mind that I am not saying this describes everyone who believes in ECT.

his mouth because Scripture affirms that "out of the abundance of the heart, the mouth speaks."[30] Rather, I was caught off-guard by a premature "amen" from someone within an arm's reach. Her remark was far more discouraging than anything the youth pastor could have said. It was almost like it was directed right at me or, better yet, for my benefit.

On the flip side of the ordeal, I have never felt such an abundance of joy than when I have shared in the fruit of my labor in sharing my convictions regarding the doctrine of Universal Reconciliation. Some time ago, I received a private message on Facebook that opened the floodgates of joy and humility. After months of estrangement, a former friend of mine sent me the following message:

> Remember me? I was on your page and we had a big debate [on] Christian Universalism vs Eternal hell? And it all ended badly? Well, now I actually agree with you on Christian Universalism. I can't see the teaching of an eternal hell in the Scriptures. Thanks for presenting this view to me, as it stuck with me for a while, nagging at me to consider. Being introduced into the church and believing eternal hell was a part of Christian doctrine is a hard hurdle to overcome. Just thought I'd give you this tidbit of encouragement. God bless you, Charles. Forgive me for my past.

For me, the only thing that surpasses witnessing someone come to the realization that God can and will draw everyone to the cross is when one of his prodigal children come home. I *long* to experience the two together. In this generation, I envision a worldwide revival built on the *really* good news of Universal Reconciliation. However, I doubt that there will be another nationwide revival, much less one that is worldwide, until CU is preached as fervently as ECT is presently defended.

I am by no means a prophet, but I foresee a time when salvation will no longer be presented primarily as a means to avoid an end.[31] I am not alone. *Many* Christians long for the day when reconciliation will no longer be motivated by threats of annihilation or of endless misery, but rather with a simple explanation of God's perpetual grace and mercy, relentless love, and victorious justice for all people.

In the grand scheme of things, we are all his sheep—either lost[32] or found. So, too, are we all his children—either prodigal or at home in his arms. Our lives have been likened unto a vapor that vanishes just as quickly

---

30. Matt 12:34b.
31. This is not to say that everyone who accepts ECT sees it like that.
32. In the following section, I will examine the claim that goats and lost sheep are synonymous terms.

as it forms.[33] In relation to eternity, our life on earth is but a dash or a comma in the celestial library of his kingdom, which is bursting at the seams with volumes upon volumes of books that are in the process of being written. When we die, it is not "THE END," but merely one section of what he has for us. It is during the largest portion of eternity, after we exhale our final earthly breath, that the character of God will matter most. Can we trust the Author and Finisher of our faith to do what is right? God help us, if we cannot.

---

33. Jas 4:1.

Section 3

The Mystery of His Will

> In him we have redemption through his blood, the forgiveness of our trespasses, according to the riches of his grace, which he lavished upon us, in all wisdom and insight making known to us the mystery of his will, according to his purpose, which he set forth in Christ as a plan for the fullness of time, to unite all things in him, things in heaven and things on earth.
>
> —EPHESIANS 1:7–10

THE FOLLOWING MAY COME as a surprise for many. And then again, it may not. Nevertheless, "the mystery of his will," as mentioned in Paul's epistle to the Ephesians, is technically *not* a mystery. Even though he uses terminology that seems to imply as much, he abruptly undercuts that notion in the same sentence in which it is used.

In 1 Peter, we are told about how the prophets of old carefully searched and inquired about "mysteries" into which even angels long to look,[1] yet the mysterious nature of his will was apparently not for them to discern. Under the Old Covenant, humanity's attempt to decipher this algorithm, of sorts, was futile. Once the fullness of times had come for God to empty himself, to take the form of a servant, and to be born in our likeness, it was finally time for him to reveal his master plan for the world. Jesus' incarnation signified that the world was finally ready for the message that only he could bring.

According to Scripture, God does not desire for humankind to remain ignorant, especially when it comes to what he has carefully hidden: "For nothing is hidden except to be made manifest; nor is anything secret except

---

1. 1 Pet 1:10–12.

to come to light."[2] Since the "mystery of his will" was, in times past, known as an unknown that was seemingly impossible to grasp, we can rest assured that it, like anything that has been "hidden," was designed to be grasped in due time.

Many have questioned whether this moment of revelation has arrived or if it is still unfolding. According to the passage above, this mystery *has* come to light. Yet many still believe that it remains cloaked in prophetic shadows. Many are not privy to accepting that this mystery has been revealed in full because that would seem to imply everything/everyone will eventually find reconciliation in Christ, which does not resonate well with many.

Predictably, Paul anticipated this reaction. He understood that people rarely respond positively to anything that challenges their presuppositions. He could relate with our tendency to explain away ideas that conflict with our preconceived notions. From the time the New Testament documents were secretly circulated by first-century converts up to this moment in time, Christians have attempted to explain away the all-inclusive nature of two words in Paul's letter to the church in Ephesus. Of all things, the two words that seem to rub Christians the wrong way are the words: all things.

Throughout Jesus' ministry, he was condemned by the religious elite for befriending the outcasts and dining with the least of these. His own apostles were even taken aback by his radical lifestyle. Jesus' understanding of the human condition was surpassed by none. The Apostle Paul was probably one of the few, in his time and ours, who could even approached the standard that Jesus set for his followers.

Considering Paul's religious upbringing, he could relate with those to whom he was writing. Therefore, as he penned each of his letters, he wrote in a manner that addressed the red flags as they appeared. In the passage above, when he penned or dictated those two words, he predicted possible contentions and reiterated the natural meaning of those words, even though it was not grammatically necessary. He demystified "all things" by paralleling it with "things in heaven and things on earth."[3] This would surely clear things up—right?

Nevertheless, Paul's redundancy was not sufficient for some.[4] The majority of respectable commentaries focus on one aspect of this passage—the inclusion of the gentiles,[5] which does not address his primary

---

2. Mark 4:22.
3. Or "heavenly" and "earthly" things.
4. This "some" became "many" over time.
5. That is, non-Jews.

message. The concept of Jesus reconciling the world to himself[6] seems to support the notion that this uniting of all things in Christ corresponds with him reconciling the entire world.[7] However, many who insist that the Bible should always be interpreted literally interpret this passage figuratively/hyperbolically. "All kinds of people" and "all kinds of things" replaces "the world" and "all things," which limits the expressive scope of God's attributes in and for the world.

***

In the time of Christ, anyone who taught that gentiles could find favor in God's eyes without converting to Judaism suffered in numerous ways. Today, Christians who believe anything that is not considered "orthodox" are, likewise, labeled as a liberal and not treated well by the orthodox crowd. Multiply this a thousandfold and you will only catch a glimpse of what Christians endured shortly after Jesus' Great Commission. Converts were forced by cultural pressures to convert to Judaism, to deny that they saw Jesus after his acclaimed resurrection, or to "admit" that Jesus did not fulfill messianic prophecies. If they refused to deny their faith, they would suffer humiliating consequences in plain sight of their friends and family—that is, if the entire household did not share in their suffering.

One of the most renowned "heresies" of the Christian religion was the claim that sinners could gain favor with God apart from legalistically keeping his Law, which included hundreds of ceremonial laws. Anyone who opposed the Old Covenant and lived their lives according to the new one suffered greatly at the hands of the religious elite, even though they did not intentionally break moral laws any more than their Jewish neighbors.[8] Nevertheless, they suffered greatly because they lived within a culture that was committed to a covenant that was described as "eternal" in Old Testament documents.[9] Imagine the outrage when Jesus claimed that he was ushering in a New Covenant, which, by implication, would replace the old. Who was he to speak as though he possessed divine authority, to act as though he had the right to do away with something that God had established? For the love of God, he even forgave sins!

---

6. 2 Cor 5:18–19.

7. Some view "the world" as hyperbole for "all kinds of people" or "Jews and Gentiles."

8. However, they began to distinguish moral laws from ceremonial ones.

9. 1 Chr 16:17.

Although Jesus plainly stated that he did not come to "do away" with the Law, but to fulfill it, many failed to realize his purpose in life. Since Israel could not fulfill the Old Covenant,[10] but violated it time and time again, Jesus came to accomplish what they could not and, thereafter, to give the kingdom of God to a new nation.[11] Part of Jesus' mission was to fulfill the law by illuminating its shadows, by cutting a new channel to direct the river to whom its water was always intended—to those for whom Christ was slain.[12]

As this section progresses, I will present God's immaculate attributes in their pristine condition and demonstrate how the doctrine of Universal Reconciliation is simply the result of following God's attributes where they naturally lead.

> Read not to contradict and confute, nor to believe and take for granted... but to weigh and consider.

---

10. Isa 24:5.
11. Matt 21:43; Acts 13:46.
12. 2 Cor 5:14; 1 John 2:2.

8

Biblically Unorthodox Faith

> A man will please God better by believing some things that are not told him, than by confining his faith to those things that are expressly said—said to arouse in us the truth-seeing faculty, the spiritual desire, the prayer for the good things which God will give to them that ask him.
>
> —GEORGE MACDONALD[1]

ONE OF THE FIRST things we are taught, as Christians, is that faith is an essential component in living a life that pleases God. However, from that point forward, many fail to realize what comes along with a lifelong faith. Somewhere along the line, many came to believe that faith and knowledge are mutually exclusive concepts—that it is impossible to have faith in what is indisputable. Although this may be a legitimate deduction from secular presuppositions, biblical presuppositions *should* discourage Christians from coming to that conclusion. If faith and knowledge[2] are mutually exclusive concepts, the reasonable Christian will eventually have to question the authenticity of the first-century converts because they were firsthand witnesses of that which, indisputably, substantiated the Christian faith.

If the Bible's portrayal of faith parallels the secularist's, the world has caught the Christian religion in a precarious position. However, since the Bible defines its own terms, as does every worldview, Christians are not required to account for contradictions that would have been unavoidable if it did not define its own terms. According to Scripture, it *is* possible to be

---

1. George MacDonald, "A Higher Faith," in *Unspoken Sermons: Series i, ii, and iii.* 2012. Kindle edition. First published 1867–89.

2. The Bible does say that we cannot hope in what is seen/known, but that is something else entirely.

confident in the veracity of our faith because faith in what is knowable is not a contradiction in terms.[3]

In John 20:29, Jesus suggested that those who believe in what they have not seen find more of a blessing in their faith than those who were eyewitnesses of the resurrection.[4] This implies that those whose faith was independently verified through their own senses possess a faith that is just as legitimate as those whose faith is not by sight. Many have suggested that saving faith is forever out of reach once someone has been presented with postmortem evidence for the validity of the biblical worldview. However, in order to remain consistent, the same would have to be said about those who have been presented with evidence for the biblical worldview on this side of the grave.[5]

However, this presupposition raises many questions, one of which regards one of Jesus' apostles whose name will forever be associated with doubt. Whether Thomas's faith was authentic when he decided to forsake the only life he had known in order to follow Jesus or if he was on the fence until he actually saw the Messiah in his glorified state, we can infer that faith, in any measure, pleases God.

Parents do not require their children to abide by a certain standard before they can find favor in their eyes. There is no checklist that children must complete before their parents will love them. Even though God wants our faith to be perfected, he does not expect a flawless faith from those who love him; at least, not in this world. Moreover, he does not expect anything, much less faith, from those who do not know him, although he desires as much. Sanctification is a relational process before our holy Father, rather than a requisite for our acceptability. It is the fruit of reconciliation, which is the fruit of faith and, in turn, the fruit of grace.

Jesus religiously taught that the smallest measure of faith is invaluable.[6] He once commended a centurion for having more faith than *all* of Israel.[7] Yet on another occasion, he rebuked his apostles for lacking it.[8] Faith was the central theme of Jesus' ministry. Even when he preached on other concepts, it always had something to do with faith in one way or another.

3. Heb 6:19.
4. John 20:29.
5. Rather than realizing that evidence actually enables us to see more clearly and, therefore, to have a will that is not as restrained as it would have been without it, many presume that our will is only free if we are in a state of ignorance. In other words, many believe that true faith requires a contorted frame of reference.
6. Matt 17:20.
7. Matt 8:10.
8. Matt 8:26.

However, he never once reacted like many Christians do today when someone does not respond positively to the gospel. If someone was not ready to follow him, he was apparently okay with that.

On one occasion, a wealthy young man walked away from Jesus after he was told what a life of faith would entail. The interesting thing about this scenario is how Jesus did not go running after the young man to warn him about the "eternal consequences" of his decision. Jesus allowed the man to walk away without any last-ditch efforts to "win" his soul. Instead, he simply warned the onlookers about how excessive wealth could be detrimental to a life of faith.

Paul's testimony may be a better example of God's unmerited favor and long-suffering than Thomas's or even the story about the rich young man. As one of the most renowned Pharisees of his day, Saul was notorious for persecuting anyone that was associated with the parasitic "Jesus movement." Even though he was one of the most prominent enemies of what Jesus called "the kingdom of God,"[9] he genuinely believed that he was serving God by purging the Holy Land of the sudden swarm of (what he saw as) antinomian renegades. He sincerely believed that he was fulfilling God's calling for his life, even though his actions were as evil as they could get.[10] Even so, God is renowned for working evil out for good.

Before Saul experienced his head-on collision with Jesus en route to Damascus, his religion involved a *pursuance* of God's favor through a legalistic adherence to the Law. Once his "old man" was laid to waste, Jesus picked up the pieces and gave him a new name that represented the birth of a new man in Christ—the Apostle Paul. Thereafter, his religion involved an *acceptance* of God's unmerited favor through faith in the obedience of Christ.

If it is impossible for anyone to have faith in what they have perceived, the greatest missionary of all[11] was faithless and was, for that reason, unable to please God.[12] If faith and knowledge are incompatible, the initial twelve, along with around five hundred others,[13] were also without faith. Yet if it *is* possible to have faith without being ignorant of the truth, one of the primary arguments against postmortem reconciliation disintegrates.

---

9. Or "the kingdom of heaven."

10. When someone's actions are evil, regardless of how genuine their intentions may be, they are no less responsible for their immorality.

11. Yes, even greater than Billy Graham.

12. Heb 11:6.

13. 1 Cor 15:6.

Faith in the Word of God

Upon conversion, Christians are given a newborn desire to trust the "plain teaching" of God's Word.[14] Since pastors generally reinforce this desire through sermons and so forth, church congregants follow their lead by encouraging each other to do likewise. Although this seems like a noble endeavor, these "clear teachings" vary from denomination to denomination. Consequently, many believers have come to trust in doctrines that are not as clearly taught in the Bible as is supposed.[15]

Salvation is not attained or withheld when someone affirms or denies some nonessential doctrine. Faith is not about believing *that* something is true as much as it is about believing *in the Truth*. It is more about the heart than it is about the head. Believing in him whom the Bible identifies as the Way, the Truth, and the Life is what imparts *aiōnion* life.

Throughout the world, or at least throughout the portion of the world with Western ideologies, it would be difficult to find a church that is reputable for teaching "sound doctrine"[16] where you will not hear, on any given Sunday morning, at least a half-dozen references to the Bible as "the Word of God."

Pastors, deacons, elders, and other authoritative figures in the church take pride in their congregation's ironclad belief in the Bible as "the inerrant, infallible, true, and trustworthy *Word* of God." If you are within earshot when this mantra echoes throughout a church's corridor, you will experience the sudden rush of adrenaline that leaves Christians in awe each and every Sunday morning. Unfortunately, many get so caught up in the moment that they tend to gloss over what would normally raise a question or two from a neutral spectator.

Have you ever asked yourself why "the Word of God" has become synonymous with "the Bible"? Does it claim to be "the Word"? In response, some may say, "I'm sure it does. Otherwise, why would we call it that?" If so, does it also claim to be the Way, the Truth, and the Life? To which, most would reply, "Of course not!" No Christian would dare to call the Bible "the Way, the Truth, or the Life," since it points sinners to he who is exclusively worthy of those titles. Yet since John 1:1 plainly states that *Jesus* has been "the Word" since the beginning,[17] is he not also exclusively worthy of that title?

---

14. In this case, I am referring to the essential doctrines of the Faith.
15. In this case, I am referring to the nonessential doctrines of the Faith.
16. This is essentially the same as saying they strictly teach that which is accepted as orthodox and eschew anything that causes dissension.
17. John 1:1.

Since "the Word" is used interchangeably with Jesus and the Bible, why is "Jesus" and "the Bible" not used interchangeably as well? When was the last time you heard someone refer to the Bible as "Jesus" or "the Son of God"? If Jesus and the Bible are certainly different entities, one of the statements above must be in error.[18] Christians could claim that they have a different understanding of "the Word" in different contexts. For instance, they could say, "Jesus is God the Word and the Bible is the Word of God." On the surface, that seems to make sense. However, it creates more issues than it attempts to resolve.

Trinitarian theology refers to Jesus as God the Son—the second person of the triune Godhead—and Scripture refers to Jesus as the Son of God. "God the Son" and "the Son of God" are apparently interchangeable terms. Therefore, this antecedent should discourage us from justifying a mistreatment of a similar set of terms.[19] Jesus is the Son of God and God the Son; he is God the Word and the Word of God. Christening the Bible with either of those titles deifies the book as the written Word; thereby, it adds a fourth entity to the triune Godhead.

Nevertheless, my argument should only be taken so far. It is no enormous error to refer to the Bible as the Word because Scripture is technically God's message or "words" to humanity. In the Old Testament, when God made a decree/promise, it was referred to as a "word" that would not return void/unfulfilled once it had gone out from his mouth in righteousness.[20] However, responsible interpreters of Scripture should consider the possible implications and connotations of their expositions before they use them because teachers of his "Word" will be judged with a greater strictness.[21]

---

18. I would like to point out that "the" in "the Word" suggests exclusivity. Two different entities cannot both be "the" anything. For example, bread and pineapple are both kinds of food. Yet bread and pineapples are not interchangeable terms. However, no one claims that bread or pineapple are "the" food because food is not an exclusive noun with only one possible pronoun. Likewise, only one person can be "the President" of a single organization—although there can be many "presidents" of numerous organizations.

19. Many disagree with the law of expositional constancy because exegesis may require an interpretation altogether different from previous usages.

20. Isa 45:23.

21. Jas 3:1–12.

Faith in God the Word

Faith expects from God what is beyond all expectation.

—ANDREW MURRAY

In response to CU, many say something like, "I would love for Christian Universalism to be true, but it's not." Or, "I would be thrilled if God could/would save everyone. Unfortunately, that's not going to happen—he can't/won't." For many, CU sounds too good to be true; it is beyond all expectation.

Biblical faith trusts. It expects. It does not merely trust in what is most clearly taught in the Bible, but it expects the best from God. To expect what is beyond all expectation is to expect what *seems* too good to be true. When something seems too good to be true, the mind that doubts the greater good makes a judgement call. It expects the lesser of two goods because it is not used to experiencing the better of two possible outcomes.

According to Murray, those who doubt that God will do the highest good should seriously work on their faith. Many Christians limit their faith by assuming: "If something sounds too good to be true, then it probably is." Unfortunately, this idea is reinforced by Christians who are committed to trusting in orthodoxy even when it conflicts with what they would otherwise expect from their good good Father. It is high time for the Church to straighten out her priorities and to reassess that which has been presupposed for as long as anyone can remember.

***

Thus far, we have reaffirmed that God finds pleasure in our faith regardless of whether it resembles the reluctant faith of Thomas or the naïve faith of a small child. George MacDonald observed that faith is not just belief in something that is out of sight, but it is also belief in something that is inaudible. It is belief apart from what is directly observed, either visually or audibly.

As we study Scripture, we glean insight from its description of God's activity in the ancient world. It possesses everything we need to know about the spiritual realm, but it does not tell us all there is to know. Many Christians mistakenly assume that anything that is not directly verified by the Bible is not reliable and is likely untrue.[22] Ironically, when someone refuses to believe anything unless it is printed on the pages of their favorite

---

22. That is simply a non sequitur.

translation, they are not acting consistently with their own presuppositions because no translation of the Bible justifies that mindset. The Bible does not claim that it is the only source of truth; neither does it suggest that anything beyond itself is necessarily unreliable.[23]

George MacDonald once suggested that "confining [one's] faith to those things that are expressly said" does not please God as much as "believing some things that are not told [us]." Moreover, what *is* expressly stated in the Bible should motivate us to have a healthy faith in what is not stated so matter of factly, but revealed through "what he has made."

Since expectations come along with faith, Christians expectantly look forward to the return of Christ. This hope is directly connected with another—that he rose from the dead. If the latter is untrue, our faith is in vain. If the former is a pipe dream, what good can come from the latter? Everything revolves around the validity of these two concepts. The latter prophecy has been fulfilled.[24] All of creation yearns for the fulfillment of the former.[25]

Paul identified our hope in the Second Coming as the Blessed Hope.[26] Its fulfillment will be the greatest event that will have ever occurred because it will lead to the consummation of God's plan for Creation. It will usher in his plan to reconcile everything in heaven and on earth,[27] which will culminate with Jesus' subjection to the Father.

Two events prerequisite the Father becoming all in all—everything to everyone. The second of which is Jesus subjecting himself to the Father. The first is like it, in that the first thing that prerequisites the Father becoming all in all is the one thing that prerequisites Jesus subjecting himself to the Father—everything will be subjected to the Son.

The beautiful thing about this prophecy is that it implies that everyone will subject themselves to Jesus in the *same* manner that Jesus will subject himself to the Father—willingly and authentically. Only then will the Father be all in all,[28] in the full sense of the term. Currently, he is all in all or "everything" to we who believe in the name of Jesus. Since everything depends on God holding it together, he could be described as all in all to the uncommitted, but only in a sense that is disregarded by the prodigal and is, therefore, incomplete. Thanks be to God that he *will* bring it to completion.

---

23. Scripture has authority over everything that conflicts with its affirmations.
24. That is, the resurrection.
25. That is, the Second Coming.
26. Titus 2:13.
27. Col 1:20.
28. 1 Cor 15:28.

Christian Universalists have coined a term that represents a concept that *is* native to the Bible, yet foreign to many Christians. It incorporates two complementary biblical concepts, both of which the church has kept separate at all costs: the Second Coming of Jesus[29] and the consummation of his plan for creation—Universal Reconciliation. "The Greater Hope" was originally the title of this section. It and "The Mystery of His Will" are essentially one and the same; the latter is directly quoted from the Bible rather than implied.

Although it is currently unorthodox, trusting in what is not directly seen or heard *is* a biblical concept. It is my growing conviction that while the Bible affirms the reality of postmortem judgment, it does not expressly say which doctrine of hell is valid. If it did, Christians would not have disagreed with such passion since the reign of Saint Augustine. As we invest more effort into studying each doctrine of postmortem judgment, our eyes will continue to open and we will begin to see that Scripture does not describe the postmortem realm as vividly as is commonly accepted.

Consider Francis Chan's evolving perspective: "The debate about hell's duration is much more complex than I first assumed. While I lean heavy on the side that says it is everlasting, I am not ready to claim that with complete certainty."[30]

As responsible followers of Jesus and/or intellectually honest individuals, we should set our presuppositions about postmortem judgment aside and allow God's attributes to lead us wherever they may. If you are ready to do just that, Chapter 9 is a page away.

---

29. That is, the Blessed Hope.

30. Francis Chan and Preston Sprinkle, *Erasing Hell: What God Said About Eternity, and the Things We Made Up* (Colorado Springs, CO: David C. Cook, 2011), 86.

9

Perpetual Grace and Mercy

> What gives me the most hope every day is God's grace; knowing
> that his grace is going to give me the strength for whatever I face,
> knowing that nothing is a surprise to God.
>
> —RICK WARREN

ACCORDING TO THE BIBLICAL worldview, grace is the means through which God expresses his presence in our lives;[1] which gives us hope. Since unbelievers do not have any hope in the grace of a God, it seems as though God's grace does not aid those who do not trust in Christ. Although it is true that the grace of God does not give unbelievers hope, it does not follow that they are unaffected by his grace.

Although I believe the hope Warren has placed in the God's grace is not misplaced or misguided, he does not seem to grasp its breadth. In order to identify the questions that have the greatest potential to illuminate the tenebrous nooks and crannies of Christian theology, in order to gain a proper understanding of the subject matter at hand, we must acknowledge two concepts—perhaps more, but let's consider two.

First of all, we must acknowledge the fact that *everyone* interprets Scripture through a set of lenses that determines their perception. If we allow our lenses to determine that any doctrine which clashes with our presuppositions is necessarily unreliable, they will become detrimental to our commitment to test all things. Consequently, they become more like a pair of blinders rather than a window through which we can properly interpret theological and philosophical propositions.

Each of us has been gifted with lenses that evolve as we experience different stages of life. They are not designed to eliminate the peripheral, but

---

1. This is similar to how the rustling of the leaves evidences the wind.

to provide an accurate depiction of our surroundings. Rather than allowing our lenses to blind us from the truth, we must remain open to experiencing a shift in perspective, which is rarely instantaneous but the byproduct of a gradual transformation of the way by which we see things.

A full-blown paradigm shift consists of numerous reassessments of seemingly incidental concepts that coalesce into a fresh way of looking at the world. Although the Christian life has been described as a race that we should strive to finish,[2] blocking out the peripheral is not necessarily advantageous. Our Jockey is not training us to dash across this strange soil with the sole purpose of getting off it as quickly as possible. Rather, he expects us to run well and to have a positive effect on those around us, which often requires slowing down to a trot or even a casual walk.

As we pass each checkpoint on this track, there are numerous obstacles that we may merely glimpse or miss entirely, depending on the condition of our lenses. If we allow them to block out the peripheral, we may end up taking the long way around something that was intended to be experienced and maneuvered. We may finish the race "successfully," but we may only do so with a sub-par performance and miss out on many of the mysteries and wonders of this world.

The second concept that we must acknowledge is no less important than the first. Rather than allowing our doctrinal convictions to contort the immutable attributes of God, of which I believe ECT is guilty, we must allow his attributes to determine the legitimacy of doctrinal propositions.[3] When it comes to theological matters, it is one thing to admit the possibility of error on our part. It is something else entirely to acknowledge that our beliefs could be erroneous *because* of faulty presuppositions. Given that much of the Bible is subject to interpretation,[4] we must suppress our urge to deem our subjective interpretation as the essential rendering of nonessential issues—"Thus sayeth the Lord!"

Although the Bible is authoritative, it does not "rightly divide the word of truth"[5] on its own. Although Scripture interprets Scripture, it does not interpret itself without an interpreter. According to the fallacy of reification,[6] the Bible does not "say" anything because documents are inanimate objects.

---

2. 2 Tim 4:7.

3. Annihilation (CI) is just as guilty, although perhaps to a lesser extent.

4. Granted, one interpretation is valid. Yet most are humble enough to admit the possibility of misinterpretation regarding that which does not qualify or disqualify anyone from salvation (nonessential doctrines). Most Christians would agree that everyone does not have to believe as they do.

5. 2 Tim 2:15.

6. Reification: to attribute a concrete characteristic to something that is abstract.

PERPETUAL GRACE AND MERCY

We carry the responsibility of dividing the word of truth responsibly, which is essential in effectively handling the Sword of the Spirit. Rather than using our fallible interpretations as replica swords of the Spirit, we must allow his immutable attributes to determine what is and is not of the Spirit.

The fourth chapter of 1 John addresses the concept of "testing spirits" as a means to determine whether or not something is of God. Regardless of how godly a Christian may appear, we can determine whether or not (s)he is of God by asking one simple question: "Does (s)he deny Jesus?" Although John was warring against Gnosticism in this epistle,[7] the instructions he offered are of value on a much larger scale. One of which regards the process of interpreting Scripture and applying it in meaningful ways. In his epistle, John encouraged his readers to "test every spirit." Therefore, we are permitted to apply his teachings and edicts beyond their immediate contexts.

So, how exactly are we to test *every* spirit? One of the most important tests that sound doctrine must pass is whether or not it denies essential truths of the Christian faith. A spirit that "confesses" Jesus may also deny him indirectly. By what method should we test the "theological spirits" per se? I propose a very simple method that believers have been using since there was Scripture to properly divide, whether preserved by scribes on parchment or stamped in the mind via oral tradition.

If two interpretations claim to confess Jesus and neither outright denies him, the only question that remains is whether or not the presuppositions behind each interpretation accurately reflect the attributes of the Most High. Unfortunately, many claim that they accept what the Bible "clearly" says about any given matter, chalking up any inconsistency to their inability to understand the things of God. In doing so, many have elevated their theological convictions to divinely inspired levels and have disregarded the insights of others if they do not align with their own.

In the quote at the beginning of this chapter, Warren claimed to be knowledgeable of two things. The first was that God would give him the strength necessary for absolutely anything that he might experience in his life. The second was similar in that while knowing/trusting in it, he could rest that much more securely in the former—that nothing is a surprise for God.[8] It is difficult to see at first glance, but he was connecting two concepts that are not often considered together, which suggests its implications are not usually explored. How is God's grace affected by his omniscience?

---

7. According to Norbert Brox, Docetism is "the doctrine according to which the phenomenon of Christ, his historical and bodily existence, and thus above all the human form of Jesus was altogether mere semblance without any true reality."

8. God is omniscient.

Certain portions of Scripture apply particularly to believers, while others apply to humankind before they come to the Faith. However, much of Scripture is applicable to both camps simultaneously. Unfortunately, there has been some contention on which passages apply to whom. Unfortunately, many have mistakenly treated God's attributes similarly. As Christians, we can focus a little too much on how the grace of God affects us, as believers, and how his omniscience comes into play in *our* lives.

Christians trust and rest in the grace of God because we *know* that it is guided by his unlimited knowledge, his omnibenevolence, and so forth. He knows us. Therefore, we feel secure in Christ. Many presume that those who do not know God are not known by him; since they do not know him, many infer that God does not know them. Jesus told his followers that a day would come when he would tell many who genuinely believed that they were his disciples that they were mistaken. Many will hear the dreadful words, "I never knew you... depart from me." With what seems to be simple logic, the uncommitted have been identified as those whose souls are excluded from the beneficiary effect of God's grace.

Many believe that the spiritual condition of the uncommitted entails a lack of grace, *due* to a lack of faith. However, Scripture teaches that salvation comes *by* grace through faith rather than the other way around. Can his grace affect those he does not know? It is true that prodigal children do not know their Father in the same way as those who remain at home, but that does not mean that the Father does not know them. As the Creator/Potter/Father of creation, God knows the prodigal as much as any father knows his rebellious children or as any shepherd knows his sheep lost in the thickets. Every soul belongs to God every bit as much as a lost coin rightly belongs to whom it is lost.

"Lost" implies ownership. God's property is known by him, even if it is not currently in his possession. Although God does not know the lost as intimately as he knows those who have been found, no one is *totally* unknown by him.[9] The Potter of the cosmos has affirmed that *everything* belongs to him. Scripture states, as a matter of fact, that *every* soul is his.[10] Nevertheless, there is undoubtedly a deeper relationship between children who are in communion with their Father than there is with prodigals who have not formally met their Paternal Sire.

Rather than allowing ECT to determine our understanding of God, let's consider what we know is true about him and determine how we ought

---

9. If the familial connection has not been reestablished, neither party enjoys a mutually beneficial relationship.

10. Ezek 18:4.

The Conciliation in Reconciliation

> The Father judges no one, but has given all judgment to the Son.
>
> —JOHN 5:22

According to this verse, it seems like the Father has nothing to do with judgment. It seems to suggest that the Father has passed this responsibility onto his Son and has chosen not to meddle with the Son's affairs. However, eight verses later, Jesus seems to contradict himself. The same Man who, in verse twenty-two, claims that the Father "judges no one" makes it abundantly clear, in verse thirty, that he can do nothing of his own; as he hears, he judges. His judgments are righteous—not just because he is righteous, but also because he selflessly seeks the righteous will of his Father. Therefore, it follows that although the Father does not judge anyone directly, he indirectly judges everyone through his Son.[11]

It feels natural to take the concept of reconciliation for granted. When was the last time *conciliation* was preached from the pulpit? Reconciliation—one step in the process of the restoration of all things[12]—is the central theme of many Sunday morning sermons. Since the Bible does not mention conciliation by name, many are only somewhat familiar with the term, much less the concept. Therefore, few have considered the scope of that which substantiates our ministry of reconciliation.[13]

Two letters distinguish one word from the other. "Re-," as a prefix, adds repetition to its root word. It also communicates a sense of unity between the subjects with which it is associated. Most people understand that reconciliation pertains to the mending of a relationship that was severed by one person or another.[14] Yet many fail to realize that reconciliation is not salvation; not entirely. Conciliation prerequisites reconciliation, which

---

11. The Son judges with the authority of the Father.
12. Acts 3:21.
13. That is, conciliation.
14. We need to be reconciled to God, not the other way around.

prerequisites salvific grace. Grace is not dependent on any merit of our own, but its *availability* is dependent on the merit of Someone.[15]

We are saved by grace through faith, not by (our) works so that no one can boast. There is one reason why we are unable to boast in our salvation—we did not *actuate* the salvation of our souls because it is impossible for the receiver of grace to be its actuator. That does not mean that grace does not have an actuator; it must. Just as an action is necessary for every reaction, a source prerequisites every action. Those who are affected by grace cannot be the cause behind the effect. Granted, grace must be received, but its reception is no more the cause of grace than the receiver of a gift is its giver. Responding in faith to grace does not actuate salvation. Rather, it *enacts* that which was actuated by he who offers reconciliation through conciliation.

Given that it is impossible for anyone to *do* anything to deserve grace, we should ask, "What motivated God to save us, to make grace available?" Many believe that everything God does is for his own glory. Although that sounds somewhat selfish, I cannot deny that there is *some* truth behind that claim.[16] Although our salvation glorifies God, I doubt that a pursuance of his own glory was or is his primary motivation behind the gospel. Salvation directly results from God's love for us, from he who is Love. Through his death, he actuated grace and is therefore credited for what naturally follows at its own pace.

In Chapter 5, we explored this concept by associating this passage with another that says, "Greater love has no man than this, than that he would lay down his life for his friends."[17] Yet Jesus laid down his life for his *enemies*.[18] He did not merely lay down his life for a small portion of his enemies who would respond in faith "before the offer expired". Rather, he laid down his life for *all* of his enemies.

Why did Jesus lay down his life? The most obvious answer pertains to his love for us, but let's focus on the implicit. His love is the substance of the answer, but there are details that often go unnoticed. Jesus did not lay down his life just because of his love for us. He also carried the cross and laid down his life for all of humanity because it was the will of his Father.[19] Those who

---

15. From the point of view of those living before the birth of Jesus, grace was dependent on what Someone Else will have done.
16. Rom 3:23.
17. John 15:13.
18. Christians were once his enemies; he was never ours.
19. John 4:34.

"saw the Son saw the Father" not just because he was God incarnate but also because "God is Christlike."[20]

***

Believe it or not, Christian Universalists are not necessarily liberalistic. Every camp has at least a few liberals in its batch. There are some liberal Christian Universalists who believe that all of humanity/creation is *already* reconciled with God. A small portion of that many puts no emphasis on the present because they believe there is nothing more that needs to be done. The larger portion of the "liberal" bunch believes that even though everyone is reconciled, each person has to come to the point where they accept, and thereby enact, their salvation. Nevertheless, I would daresay that the larger portion of Christian Universalists are not liberal and disagree with the minority regarding the *present* reconciliation of all people.

If everything has already been reconciled/subjected to Jesus, we would be living in the New Jerusalem,[21] which is obviously not a present reality.[22] Given that everyone is not presently subjected to Christ, it follows that the entire lot has not been reconciled. When Jesus said, "It is finished!", he was not saying all things were reconciled then and there. He was declaring that all prophecy regarding the first coming of the Messiah had been accomplished, disregarding his coming resurrection. He was saying the New Covenant had been enacted and that the Old Covenant was in the process of passing away—of being made obsolete.

As Jesus hung on the cross, he bridged the chasm between God and humanity. He actuated the means by which all *could* cross the chasm, but he did not enact our reconciliation because his prodigal children still have to traverse the wilderness in order to come home on their own accord. He completed his part in the process of reconciliation–conciliation. Thereafter, he gave us the ministry of reconciliation.

This is important to understand—not only for those who accept UR, but also for those who have been conditioned to reject it, not to mention those who outright reject the existence of God for reasons this book explores. I am writing to those who do not believe in Jesus and are therefore not privy to the methodology of reconciliation. I am writing no less so to Christians who reject the doctrine of UR and who might, therefore, take my

---

20. Santo Calarco.
21. Rev 21.
22. That is, unless that passage is spiritualized, which full-Preterists attempt to do.

description of reconciliation with a grain of salt. If you decide to investigate CU after reading this book,[23] you will be surprised that it is not as alien to basic biblical premises as you may have been told.

The schism between "orthodox" Christians, which is actually between Calvinists and Arminians, has been alive and well for as long as anyone can remember. Due to how long the two have been at odds, with no apparent victory on either side, there is evidently something off about that which has fueled their dissension. This schism has made little to no progress toward a resolution because neither camp has identified or acknowledged the single possibility that can permit resolution. Each camp agrees that both paradigms cannot be true at the same time, which seems to imply that one of the two must be false. Yet neither seems to have considered the possibility that neither is true, that there is a third contender.

Some Calvinists believe that Jesus died for everyone, but only the Elect will respond in faith because they are the remnant that he chose beforehand to save; while others believe that Jesus died solely for the Elect. Both, of which, believe that the Elect are reconciled when they receive faith by grace.[24] They believe that God's grace is new every morning, but *only* for the Elect. The non-Elect are simply not chosen. Therefore, they do not benefit from his grace.

Arminians believe that Jesus died for everyone; some, of which, believe that reconciliation pertains to everyone in one way or another—that all are reconciled, but each must respond in faith to enact what Jesus accomplished on the cross for them. However, the death of the uncommitted has more power than the death of Jesus because their death makes Jesus' death null and void if they fail to respond to the call before they die.

Due to how horrible that sounds, many rightfully deny that Jesus' feat is null and void for anyone, but that is exactly where Arminian theology leads—toward absurdity, because they believe that Jesus has not accomplished anything for those who die unrepentant. Like some Calvinists, some Arminians have *indirectly* disregarded the finished work of Jesus by claiming that he only died for those who respond in faith before death. They use foreknowledge as a means to justify the horrendous end for most people, while Calvinists appeal to God's inherent right to choose who to save.

Christian Universalists believe that Jesus died for everyone. Likewise, we seek to preserve the value of Jesus' work on the cross in our own manner. While Calvinists believe that grace is only applicable to those predestined

---

23. You can find a list of books that have been beneficial in my search for the truth in Appendix D.

24. Yet in the grand scheme of things, from God's point of view, they were reconciled from the foundation of the world.

to respond in faith, and Arminians believe that grace is nearly unlimited in scope as it nears its date of expiration, Christian Universalists believe that grace is available for everyone and perpetually so.

Nothing is a Surprise for God

> Declaring the end from the beginning, and from ancient times things that are not yet done, saying, 'My counsel shall stand, and I will do all my pleasure.'
>
> —ISAIAH 46:10

Omniscience is one of God's most fundamental attributes. Although there are some Open Theists who believe that his knowledge is not unlimited, it is generally accepted that his knowledge has no borders. Although an appeal to the masses does not substantiate the legitimacy of any concept, arguing one way or the other for or against the vastness of God's knowledge would be little more than a distraction at this point.[25]

Christians affirm that nothing is a surprise for God, but many have failed to take this concept to its logical limit. This can be seen in the prevalent understanding of postmortem judgment. If we reduced the concept of omniscience to its logical limit, we would ultimately arrive at something far better than the endless misery of any portion of humankind—all of whom God deemed it good to create, by the way. We do not have to rely on just one of his attributes to reach this conclusion.

To what extent did God's grace affect us prior to our conversion? Is it true that the unrepentant do not experience the grace of God until they are saved? The fact of the matter is that God's grace is by no means one-dimensional. The multidimensional grace of God is boundless and is just one attribute of he who is no respecter of persons. Certain aspects of his grace are applicable only to those who are in the necessary condition to experience them. Yet there is much more to grace than what we experience in faith.

God's grace affects everyone, but only as far as their spiritual condition permits. Those like Rick Warren and Billy Graham experience his grace on a much higher level than those on the spiritual level of Richard Dawkins or

---

25. Those who claim that divine foreknowledge is incompatible with human freedom often explain the concept of omniscience as knowing all that is possible to know. Since it is not possible to know what a future free choice will be, they say, God's not knowing this is compatible with his omniscience.

Bill Nye. Just as those who are physically immature do not experience life to the extent that they will fifty years from now, those who are spiritually immature do not experience spiritual life to the extent that they could if they had accumulated spiritual wisdom.

Christians believe that every breath we take is given by grace. It could be said that we are breathing in grace. Unfortunately, most Christians believe that this concept has no meaning apart from irrevocable postmortem consequences—that there is no real point in life before death if we can receive grace after a lifetime of refusing it. The problem with this way of thinking is in its contorted perception of grace.

As mentioned, grace is, and must be, unmerited. The two major ways of thinking about grace have to do with the concept of free will. One of which is that God provides life as a continuous opportunity to pursue reconciliation with him. It presupposes that grace will not always be available. If that is true, the love of God is not unfailing for those who die unrepentant because the unfailing nature of his love is contingent on the perpetual newness of his grace. If his grace expires, the unfailing nature of his love vanishes with it.

It is generally assumed by Christians that everyone experiences a general sense of grace in this life. Yet the term "general" implies that there is a special kind of grace. Calvinists believe this "special" kind of grace is exclusively for the few that have been especially chosen, while Arminians believe that it is for those who are fortunate enough to realize and act on their need for redemption before they die. Calvinists believe that God chooses whom he desires to bring to their senses, while Arminians believe God desires to bring everyone to their senses but leaves the choice up to them.

Does the Bible speak of a special kind of grace? Surely not! The grace that allows rain to fall on the just and on the unjust is the same grace through which God expresses his unfailing love for everyone. Grace is not something that is offered in light of endless postmortem repercussions. The Bible never presents the gospel with threats of eternal harm.[26] Perfect love casts out *all* fear. Fear does not produce love; fear produces fear. The fear/holy reverence of the Lord is the beginning of wisdom, but love is undoubtedly its end.[27]

---

26. Rom 2:4.
27. 1 John 4:18.

10

Relentless Love

> And above all these put on love, which binds everything together in perfect harmony.
>
> —COLOSSIANS 3:14

THROUGHOUT THE BIBLE, LOVE is progressively identified as the nucleus around which every "good thing" revolves. Paul described love as the greatest of all virtues,[1] which had to do with how Jesus said it is the only means through which the Law can be—or should I say, "has been"—fulfilled.[2]

During one of the numerous instances in which Jesus was tested by the religious elite of his day, he was challenged to identify "the greatest commandment". Since he understood the intent of their hearts, he quoted Scripture: "You shall love the Lord your God with all your heart and with all your soul and with all your mind. This is the great and first commandment."[3] He went on to say that the second was like it: "to love your neighbors as you love yourself."[4] *All of the Law and Prophets depend on these two commandments.*[5]

Jesus believed that the two were so inseparable that if anyone claimed to love God while hating their brother,[6] then they were a liar[7] through and through. Therefore, it is fair to say that loving others is the byproduct of loving God—and that love toward God is the byproduct of authentic faith. The Law and the Prophets are fulfilled in this one commandment because

---

1. 1 Cor 1:13.
2. Rom 13:10; Gal 5:14.
3. Matt 22:37–38; Deut 6:5.
4. Matt 22:39; Lev 19:18.
5. Matt 22:40; 7:12; Rom: 13:10; 1 Tim 1:5–7.
6. That is, their neighbor, or even their "enemy."
7. 1 John 4:20.

if we *truly* love, we will not sin against God or anyone else. To take it a step further, it stands to reason that all sin is a consequence of a failure to love in one way or another.

According to Scripture, "Love bears all things, believes all things, hopes all things, and endures all things. Love never ends."[8] This same love that "never ends" also "binds *everything* together in perfect harmony." Apart from love, disharmony is inevitable.

Although it is not difficult to see how the concept of love binding "all things together" applies to general circumstances in life, its applicability to the abstract is not as easy to grasp. If love truly binds *everything* together, should it not also binds the intricacies of sound theological systems together as well? If a theological/philosophical system is not relentlessly bounded together with love, it will eventually burst at its seams and/or prevent its adherents from living up to their responsibility to love.

God's love for the world has existed from the beginning of time and will continue forevermore.[9] On philosophical and theological grounds, this love is *necessarily* relentless; not because of anything that we could do or have done, but simply because of who he is. Like his other attributes, his love is not constrained by time or by any other factor. Nothing about it is due to expire or subject to entropy. If it or any of his attributes were finite, they would conflict with his deity and would be, by definition, not quite divine.

Many see love as an unreliable feeling that comes and goes like waves of the sea—more like infatuation than unadulterated love. Contrarily, the Bible portrays love as an unshackled commitment to the well-being of another. Gary Thomas writes, "When the Bible commands us to love, it says nothing about what we describe as 'in love' love. Biblical love isn't a feeling to be felt, it's a commitment to be kept."[10]

I have asked several friends of mine, who believe in ECT, "If ECT is true, how does God express his unfailing love to those who are currently in hell?" Their responses were similar, if not identical. My Arminian friends did not deny God's love for all, but each one qualified his love with a confident, yet predictable, "But. . . we have free will!" Do we have free will? Yes, of course we do, but that does not answer the question. I should have asked, "In what tangible way does God express his unfailing love to those in hell?"

Few would deny that the uncommitted remain in the scope of God's love here and now. Yet why do so many Christians believe that his love ends

---

8. 1 Cor 13:7–8.

9. Cf. 1 John 4:19.

10. He goes on to say, "A lifelong love doesn't mean a lifelong infatuation." Gary Thomas, *A Lifelong Love: How to Have Lasting Intimacy, Friendship, and Purpose in Your Marriage* (Colorado Springs, CO: David C. Cook, 2014), 264.

at the gates of hell? They may deny that the residents of hell are not loved by God, but as I have and will argue, unfailing love is present-perfect. It must be expressed perpetually in order to remain unfailing. If anything changes on the other side of the grave, it must be on God's side rather than on ours. Since God is the same yesterday, today, and forever,[11] could it be that his love does not change, that he is ever-pursuant, and will never give up on anyone?

God expressed[12] his unfailing love for humanity through Jesus' death on the cross. His suffering was not reserved for those who will, or even might, come to believe in him *before* they die—although many would argue otherwise in an effort to justify the shortcomings of their presuppositions. Many believe that salvation is *potentially* for everyone, but few of that many believe that it is *actually* for everyone.[13]

Some Christians believe that Jesus died for the Church. Although that is true in a sense, there is not a consensus on what that means. One side[14] pictures Christ dying for the Church—all who will freely believe before they die. The other side[15] pictures Christ dying for the Church—certain individuals whom he chose to save before they die. According to CU theology, Christ died for everyone and will save the entire lot in the fullness of times.[16] We prefer stating that Jesus died for the world, rather than for the Church.[17] If we were to make such a statement, our understanding of this concept would be something like this: Christ died for the Church, which will eventually consist of everyone.

Since there is no potentiality with God,[18] Arminians cannot resort to saying, "Jesus died for everyone. Therefore, everyone is *potentially* a part of the Church." As far as we know, everyone can "potentially" believe before they die, but that statement is not realistic. No one's belief is potential in light of eternity, but guaranteed because God cannot fail. Theoretically, anyone can disbelieve forever; realistically, no one can.

God's ultimate will is not restrained by *anything*, especially time. Either Jesus *actually* died for everyone and all will be saved or he did not die

---

11. Heb 13:8.
12. This is the past tense.
13. With God, there is no such thing as potentiality.
14. That is, Arminians.
15. That is, Calvinists.
16. I am not suggesting the date of everyone's salvation has been predestined. God does not have to appoint the moment of anyone's salvation in order to predetermine it. By "predetermine", I mean that God decides beforehand *that* he will save them (all) when they freely succumb to his relentless love.
17. The former is actually a biblical statement; the latter is not.
18. Omniscience counteracts potentiality.

for everyone and all will not be saved.[19] If the latter is true, his love is not unfailing and definitely not relentless for those he loved and lost. Jesus did *not* die for the few who will, or even might, believe. Rather, he died for the many who died in the first Adam so that they *could/would* be raised to new life in the Second.

The Substance of God's Love

> There is no fear in love, but perfect love casts out fear. For fear has to do with punishment, and whoever fears has not been perfected in love.
>
> —1 JOHN 4:18

Seeing how God is love and a consuming fire,[20] it follows that his judgements are motivated by his love toward those who are enslaved by sin.[21] Although it is "a terrifying thing to fall into the hands of the living God," a correct perspective reveals that his judgments should be welcomed as discipline because they are always for our own good. In the heat of the moment, discipline invokes fear; from hindsight, the only thing to fear is fear itself.

***

"Hate the sin, not the sinner." Many Christians claim to live or die by this creed. Although few would not deny that Jesus lived and died accordingly, many refuse to believe that he rose and lives by it. Thanks to some chalky translations of a few passages, many have discerned that God hates the sinner as much as he hates their disease. Is this true? There is something deep within all of us that certainly hopes not. The renowned passage about God "loving" Jacob, but "hating" Esau, has long since fueled the debate. Since many books and articles have been compiled on this passage alone, I will not dig any deeper than is required to make my point.

Some have argued that God was actually talking about nations rather than individuals. Others focus on terminology and have discovered a correlation between this passage and the one where Jesus said that we must

---

19. I will expound on this assertion in the following chapter.
20. Both, of which, are unquenchable.
21. If we were to subtract God's loving nature from his actions, he would appear to suffer from schizophrenia.

hate our parents, and even our lives, if we are serious about following him.[22] Many have concluded that love and hate are semantically equivalent to "preference" in this and other contexts. In comparison, our love for Jesus should make the love we have for others look like hate to passersby. Likewise, God's favor for [the nation of] Jacob makes his lack of favor for [the nation of] Esau seem like hate when, in actuality, it has nothing to do with love versus hate, but favor versus disfavor.

God may favor one over another regarding the plans he has for the world, but his love is absolutely impartial and unconditional for everyone. According to Thomas Talbott, "All human sinners are equal objects of God's redemptive love, in my sense, only if God loves Esau every bit as much as he loves Jacob; only if he desires that Esau eventually achieve eternal happiness every bit as much as he desires that Jacob achieve eternal happiness; and only if losing Esau forever would thwart his redemptive love every bit as much as losing Jacob forever would have thwarted it."[23]

***

Just when I thought I heard it all, a friend of mine said something that baffled me. During a discussion in which I asked him about how God expresses his love for those who have died unsaved, he conceded that God loves everyone. Yet, in defense of his presuppositions, he was forced to claim that God does not love everyone *equally*.[24] It took me a moment to process this statement.

Since I had Arminian inclinations when I believed in ECT, I believed that God loved everyone *equally*. I was aware that things were not so black and white through the Calvinist's lenses, but my friend was anything but a Calvinist. How could he believe that God loves some people differently than others without abandoning the Arminian paradigm?

He explained: *As a Christian, I am called to love. The Bible instructs believers to love their neighbors; yes, even their enemies. As parents, however, we have a "special" kind of love for our children. The love we have for our family is different than the love we have for our friends—much different than love for our enemies or even strangers.*

22. Luke 14:26.

23. Thomas Talbott, *The Inescapable Love of God*, 2nd ed. (Eugene, OR: Cascade, 2014), chapter 4.

24. Jonathan Edwards and Hermann Hoeksema, have explicitly stated the same thing.

That is true enough, but does the Bible support such reasoning? Does Scripture call us to surpass these limitations? The Bible does not command us to love without *also* providing a clear explanation of what that means. Otherwise, we would be left with room to determine the scope of our love for particular classes of people. Scripture clarifies what manner of love we *should* have for our neighbors/enemies—to love, indiscriminately, as we love *ourselves*. Granted, some people do not have much love for self, but Scripture does not take that into consideration when it calls us to love because it presupposes the ideal.

Does God love some people differently from others? Apparently, some passages seem to support that idea. The Jacob and Esau narrative would be the go-to passage for anyone looking to substantiate this claim. The nation of Israel could also seem to support the notion because Scripture identified Israel as a nation that was set apart from all others; they *were* his chosen race. Yet does this support the notion that God loves some people differently than others?

If we consider how God had a unique preference for Israel, it could seem like God loved them *more* than any other nation. His favor toward her was unique in its time, just as his favor toward the Church is unique in ours. Nevertheless, the theocracy of the Old Testament has not transferred to the New Testament era as perfectly as some may have hoped. First-century Jews were, in fact, expecting that very thing as they were certain that the Savior was going to rule with an iron fist in their favor. Yet to their surprise, he came to rule with a golden tongue, which resulted in their hearts of stone.[25]

As a result of the hardness of their hearts, their birthright was to be taken away and given to another—a new nation; a royal priesthood; his *true* chosen nation; the *true* Israel; the remnant that would consist of Jews and gentiles; no, for in Christ there is neither Jew nor Greek, neither male nor female, no distinguishing factor between those who are truly the children of Abraham—the children of faith.

God never loved the physical descendants of Abraham any more than the Gentiles. His love for the descendants of Adam is everlasting to everlasting. Just like anyone could become a part of the nation of Israel, under the Old Covenant, through subjecting themselves to the ceremonial and moral laws to which Israel had sworn at the foot of Sinai,[26] so, too, can anyone become a member of his body by grace through faith in Christ.

Ever since God breathed life into the nostrils of Adam, there has been a covenant of love. The Fall did not stifle his love for the world. Rather,

---

25. For the most part.
26. Exod 19:8.

our enslavement to sin has fueled his disdain for our sinful condition; not because it tied his hands, but because it shackled our hearts. God does not desire to cast the diseased into an eternal quarantine. Rather, he longs to relieve all of creation from its birth pangs, to deliver us from our infirmities, to truly set us free.

Love is a decision. God created us because he is love. Seeing the end from the beginning, before we lost our way, he decided to empty himself, to take the form of a servant, and to be born in the likeness of mankind[27]. . . all to reconcile *us* back to himself—not the other way around. There is something about *us* that separates us from him. There is *nothing* about him that separates him from us: "For I am sure that neither death nor life, nor angels nor rulers, nor things present nor things to come, nor powers, nor height nor depth, nor anything else in all creation, will be able to separate us from the love of God in Christ Jesus our Lord."[28]

Since Paul was writing to Christians in Rome, Calvinists, in particular, argue that God's unquenchable love is exclusively for the Elect. I would like to suggest otherwise. Although it is true that Paul was speaking to and about Christians, that does not limit its scope. Earlier in this chapter, Paul wrote, "He who did not spare his own Son but gave him up for us all, how will he not also with him graciously give us all things?"[29] Again, this may appear to apply solely to the recipients of this letter, but the context of Scripture at large disallows us from saying that Jesus was "given up" for a small portion of the world.

Jesus died for the *entire* world because of God's relentless love for us all. If he did not love those who were either not predestined/foreordained to be saved or not "foreknown" in the Arminian sense, then why go through the trouble to die for those he did not predestine/foreknow? Why would God send his Son to die for those he hated or "loved differently"? Why would he send his Son to die for those he would not or could not save?

Many deny that God loves everyone equally, while some deny that he loves many at all. Many within this many claim that God loved humanity at the beginning, but grew to hate them as they turned from him. Many believe that his love rekindles for humanity once they are adopted into his family. Contrarily, this is just the opposite of the picture that Jesus painted in the parable of the prodigal son and elsewhere.

Since God is love and love is a decision to commit to the well-being of another, then we should expect something much holier from God than the

---

27. Phil 2:5–7.
28. Rom 8:38–39.
29. Rom 8:32.

diluted and selfish affection that we observe from those around us. Rather than marveling in the light of God's love, it has become something that needs to be defended in light of the "just and necessary" consequence of sin. Since when does love consist of negativity that requires a defense? If anything, we should defend its height, depth, and breadth rather than its supposed shallowness.

11

Victorious Justice

A bruised reed he will not break, and a smoldering wick he will not quench, until he brings justice to victory.

—MATTHEW 12:20

REGARDLESS OF WHERE WE reside in this world, one of the first things we learn as children is what it means to be victorious. Our competitive nature assures that we will understand victory long before we are old enough to read the word in print. Justice is also a basic human concept. One of the most common phrases among children, and many adults, is- "That's not fair!". Regardless of our physical or spiritual level of maturity, everyone has a deep need for justice.

Matthew 12:20 says justice *will* be brought to victory. What does that mean? Is that just a crafty way of saying "to succeed in bringing about justice"? Could it mean something more? How should "victory" affect our understanding of God's allocation of justice?

In earlier chapters, I proposed that all of God's attributes are mutually *inclusive*. If they are, then it follows that each expression of any particular attribute of his is, in one way or another, an expression of the entire lot. Although Chapter 12 will delve further into this concept, in this chapter we will examine it, in part, as it pertains to justice and to the apparent victory toward which it is[1] brought.

At the beginning of this passage, there may be a piece of information that could shed some light on the subject matter. The verse prior to the one which states that "he will bring justice to the nations,"[2] is stated in much less ambiguous terms. There is more to bringing justice to victory than simply

---

1. Or "will be."
2. Matt 12:18; Isa 42:1.

bringing justice to the nations. Victory is not simply about the allocation of justice. It also has to do with the manner in which justice is brought toward victory.

Regardless of how many laws we have broken or the severity of the consequences that our actions deserve, the *problem* behind it all is, by far, much more catastrophic.[3]

The Problem

According to a common moral and natural law, regardless of whether our deeds are good or evil, we should reap according to what we have sown. If we do good, we *should* reap good. If we do evil, we *should* reap evil. When we fail to reap according to what we have sown, one way or the other, justice is due.[4]

Although there are individual consequences for each of our sins, the general wage of sin is death. On the day that Adam and Eve consumed fruit from the forbidden tree, their spiritual life withered—they no longer "knew God."[5] Thenceforth, their descendants were born out of spiritual wedlock. They were born in sin and therefore experienced essentially the same consequence as he[6] who caused sin to enter the world—spiritual disunity.

Praise be to God that his love for us has never been based on our actions or lack thereof! We often hear those who accept the doctrine of ECT say, "God is love, *but* he is also just!" God *is* just, but he is not exclusively just. His attributes are multidimensional, interdependent, and harmonious. His justice is no less loving, graceful, or merciful than those attributes are just. According to George MacDonald, "Justice and mercy are simply one and the same thing; without justice to the full there can be no mercy, and without mercy to the full there can be no justice." The same goes for mercy and love.

Believers and unbelievers alike tend to associate justice with revenge. Regardless of anyone's worldview, when someone is wronged in one way or another, we generally feel like everyone should "get what's coming to them." Throughout the Psalms, David fervently cries out for justice. Rather than

---

3. This is a paraphrase of Paul Leverenz.

4. If we look at this from the perspective of business, those who are outside of Christ are in the red and are, therefore, in desperate need of a spiritual audit. Once the uncommitted seriously consider where they stand in their spiritual account, they *should* realize that they are hopelessly drowning in debt and in need of a Jubilee, which is relative to each person and can only be convened in Christ. (Isa 61:1–2; Luke 4:18–19)

5. John 17:3.

6. Rom 5:12.

imploring for the salvation of his enemies, his prayers usually pertain to their demise.

If you have never meditated on the Psalms, you will be surprised at some of the requests David lifts up to God; that is, unless you sympathize with them. Right alongside beautiful words of praise and adoration, he pleaded for the undoing of those who were against him, seemingly in ignorance of the teachings of Christ, which were derived from Old Testament teachings and ultimately from the heart of God.

Since the Son and the Father are one,[7] why was David's heart for his enemies unlike Jesus'? Some claim that since he was "a man after God's own heart," we are given a glimpse of God's heart through David's writings. If they are correct, then we are faced with a misalignment between the heart of the Father and the heart of the Son.

Although David *was* a man after God's own heart, his perspective was limited. He could not grasp the bigger picture any more than the angels, prophets, or priests of the OT could grasp what Paul identified as "the mystery of his will." Although David's heart reflected God's heart toward evil, his perspective was just as finite as anyone else's.

Our natural reaction toward injustice is to seek revenge, either directly or indirectly, on those who have done us or our loved ones wrong. Even though anger can lead us to seek revenge, anger is not necessarily a negative feeling. One of Paul's objectives in his letter to the church of Ephesus was to tell them that anger is no more of a sin than is money the root of all evil. The *love* of money is the root of *all kinds* of evil and unbridled anger is the bastard child of hate and contempt.[8]

George MacDonald once stated, "In a good man at least, 'Revenge is' as Lord Bacon says, 'a kind of wild justice,' and is easily satisfied. The heart's desire upon such a one's enemy is best met and granted when the hate is changed into love and compassion." In the Greek language, "there is a difference between revenge and punishment; the latter (*kolasis*) is inflicted in the interest of the sufferer, the former (*timōria*) is in the interest of him who inflicts it, that he may obtain satisfaction."[9] God obtains satisfaction in the latter (*kolasis*) because it achieves his will by afflicting the "sufferer" for the interest of both parties.[10] With that being said, it is also important to note

---

7. John 10:30.
8. Eph 4:26a.
9. Aristotle, *Rhetoric*, bk. 1, ch. 10, sec. 17.
10. It is difficult to realize what is in our best interest in the midst of suffering.

that "in all Greek secular literature, *kolasi*s is never used of anything but remedial punishment."[11]

When we pursue vengeance on our own accord, we deny that Jesus will bring justice to victory; we say, "I don't trust God to fulfill his promises. I will take care of it myself." If we choose to leave vengeance in God's hands, we will deny the lust of the flesh and wait patiently on his timing. Many have attempted to justify their contempt by convincing themselves that God uses *them* as vessels of wrath as they dish out justice as *they* see it. Yet when all is said and done, the avenger usually feels no better than before.

Many fail to realize that justice is not solely about the righting of a wrong. The means toward that end is just as important as the end. True justice pursues vindication as it seeks to resolve something else entirely—the root cause of it all. When *we* seek revenge, we are usually driven by our ego, which demands that *we* get what *we* deserve when *we* deserve it.[12]

As Christians, we are called to repay evil with good, rather than with evil or even indifference. This calling is much more than a command we have been given. It is also a *desire* with which we have been blessed. The Christian faith yields a desire to follow our charge to *overcome* evil with good.[13]

Pond Scum Theology

> "Pond-scum theology makes even less sense in the context of the Gospels. To believe that people are inherently worthless to God strips the incarnation, crucifixion, and resurrection of all their meaning and power. It makes Jesus look like a fool for dying for us, and it leaves behind his followers with little incentive to seek out and celebrate the good in one another."
>
> —RACHEL HELD EVANS [14]

Are people inherently worthless? Some Christians believe so; others do not. I would like to suggest that if ECT is true, people must be inherently worthless. Otherwise, God would never abandon those who are inherently

---

11. William Barclay, *A Spiritual Autobiography* (Grand Rapids, MI: Eerdmans, 1977), 66.

12. Some question whether or not we deserve anything at all.

13. 1 Pet 3:9; Rom 12:17–21.

14. Rachel Held Evans, *Evolving in Monkey Town: How a Girl Who Knew All the Answers Learned to Ask the Questions* (Grand Rapids, MI: Zondervan, 2010), 117.

priceless. If we are of no value outside of Christ, why would God bother giving us a conscience or a system of moral laws for which we are accountable? Inherently worthless creatures are no less worthless if they know the difference between good and evil and choose the former. If we are only of value to God if we are in Christ, what motivated him to send his Son to lay down his life for the world in the first place? We cannot be loved and worthless at the same time because love evidences inherent worth; so, too, does grace and mercy.

One of the primary doctrines of the Christian faith, or so we have been told, says that Jesus *had* to die in our place in order to *appease* the vindictive nature of the Father.[15] We are taught that if we die before we repent of our sins and commit our lives to Jesus, then *we* will have to "pay" the penalty for our sins, which entails, according to prevalent presuppositions, everlasting torment with no hope of grace, mercy, or love—with a little less emphasis on a lack of love, for some reason.

Since there is apparent tension between the all-encompassing love of God and ECT's notion of justice, many have been forced to admit that God somehow expresses love there. When I accepted this doctrine, I was never forced to wrestle with this conundrum. Until recently, many Christians could relate. However, the average churchgoer is now being held accountable much more consistently by other Christians and unbelievers alike for their theological convictions—as they should.

Many who are aware of the tension between the love of God and ECT's portrayal of justice have been forced to claim that God expresses his love to the lost *by* sending them to hell, even though it is not for their better good. Since some claim that God does not *send* anyone to hell, but that people "choose" to go there by rejecting Jesus, I will rephrase this statement using accepted terminology: "Many who are aware of the tension between the love of God and ECT's portrayal of justice have been forced to claim that God expresses his love to the lost by *casting them* into a place where they will experience unbearable agony for ever and ever and ever."[16]

The only means by which one can acknowledge that God expresses his love to those in hell is by claiming that he expresses his love for them by "giving them what they want," which is, in this case, "nothing to do with him." This suggests, however, that those who die unrepentant will never want anything to do with God even when their misconceptions are out of the way and that they prefer to suffer forever over being comforted; not

---

15. This is the doctrine of penal substitution.
16. Rev 20:15.

to mention that postmortem judgment is, theoretically, designed to harden their hearts rather than to soften them.

***

Have you ever wondered *how* Jesus "paid" for our sins if our debt requires ECT or annihilation? He did not suffer endlessly in hell; neither was he annihilated. He was only dead for *three* days, after all. Did he get out on parole because of good behavior? Was endless conscious torment or annihilation not required because of his innocence? The fact of the matter is that he *was* guilty because he *actually* took on the sins of the entire world—he *actually* "became sin for us."[17]

I have often asked myself, "Why was the death of Jesus *required* for the remission of my sins?" I have been told a number of things. The primary evangelical response to this question pertains to our inability to pay our own sin-debt before God, regardless of the length and magnitude of the consequences. The problem with this answer is that it assumes that our worth and acceptability before God depends on whether or not we are in Christ, even though intrinsic worth is not dependent on relative conditions of the heart. In the same breath, we are told that grace has nothing to do with what we do or do not owe God. Salvation is about resting in his unmerited favor, we are told. Yet if we are unable to appease God regardless of what we experience in postmortem dungeons, what's the point of it all? Is God chomping at the bit to exact revenge?

Christians assume that God's "vengeance" corresponds with their particular view of postmortem judgment. The prevalent opinion on the matter presupposes ECT is indisputable since most Christians assume that it is simply what the Bible teaches. "Who are you, O man, to question God? His ways are not our ways. His thoughts are not our thoughts." Indeed, God's ways and thoughts are not our ways or thoughts. They are, by far, much *better*. His ways and thoughts are much more loving, merciful, graceful, and just than the best of our intentions. They are altogether holier.[18]

Skeptics are not able to buy into the popular evangelical explanation of the gospel because it is difficult to follow leaps in logic. Why would God punish us if the punishment could never suffice—for mere justice? Moreover, why would he sovereignly will any number of conscious souls into

---

17. 2 Cor 5:21.
18. See Isaiah 55.

suffering of any kind if their discomfort does not redirect their ways, as is its purpose in life (disregarding the life/death sentence)?[19]

Are we supposed to blindly accept the claim that Jesus came to temporarily suffer a permanent punishment in our place? Why was the death of Jesus required for the remission of our sins? Was it? I cannot say with certainty that it was "required," but, as a Christian, I cannot deny that it was necessary. Why was it necessary? Now, *that* is the question.

***

Theologians have identified Israel as a shadow or type of its New Testament antitype—the Church. Therefore, many are uncomfortable with making any connections or applications beyond that which has been established. The "Written Word" is full of gems that are waiting to be found if we would go the extra mile, if we would dig just a little bit deeper. I have sat through many sermons and lectures that sounded like the pastor or teacher was just a couple steps away from proclaiming the really good news of Universal Reconciliation—only if they would have taken what they were saying just a little bit further and connected what they were saying about justice with their claims about God's love, grace, and mercy.

How would you react if I claimed that Israel can represent humanity as a whole without denying the analogy that identifies the Church as her antitype? Many would find that shocking and maybe even heretical because the world is often contrasted to, rather than compared with, Israel. However, since this analogy does not reject the other or deny its validity, there is no reason to overreact. Rest assured, I have no desire to crossbreed two separate species.

The following analogy may be a stretch, but bear with me for a moment; it may not. This idea came to me when I was reading about Israel's time of slavery in Egypt. Since the Bible parallels our sinful condition with slavery,[20] it is fitting to parallel Egypt with our sinful condition. Since Israel was enslaved in Egypt, she naturally lines up with the human race since humanity is "a slave to sin."

As a type of the Christ/Messiah, Moses often spoke face-to-face with God, intervened on Egypt's behalf, and validated his prophetic office

---

19. The life sentence has an end in view, at which point the prisoner is given fully into the hands of he who is better equipped to achieve what is impossible with humankind. With humans, reformation may not be possible; but with God, any good thing is possible.

20. John 8:34; Rom 6:6.

through signs and wonders. Israel/humankind was not created to live in slavery/the sinful condition in which they found themselves. They/we were originally *free*, in every meaningful sense of the term.

It was not until Israel moved to Egypt, like the human race was casted from Eden, that their road to slavery begun. Israel's road to slavery began when Joseph's brothers sold him into slavery.[21] Granted, what they intended for evil, God intended for good. Yet the broader consequences for their actions were not fully realized until generations after their "original sin."

Hundreds of thousands of people were born into slavery because of the actions of the original patriarchs of eleven tribes of Israel.[22] They toiled by the sweat of their brow and could not escape their harsh taskmaster.[23] They were trapped in a lifestyle that they never dreamt of leaving and eventually had forgotten their heritage.[24] Any thought of redemption was as foreign to them as was the Good News that Jesus delivered to the world.

The only thing they were familiar with at the point of their messiah's (Moses) appearance was work—toiling by the sweat of their brow. When he suddenly arrived with an unfamiliar message of hope, they were anything but supportive; that is, until he began to prove himself through signs and wonders. Initially, Moses's message increased their tribulation, but, when all was said and done, they traversed the Red Sea/the narrow road toward the Land of Promise. Moses came to set God's people free, but Israel had to have faith in the promises of God in order for their destiny to be realized.

Generations after Moses died, Israel was taken into captivity. The two southern tribes of Israel, who were called the house of Judah, returned to their land. Yet the northern ten tribes, who were called the house of Israel, "never came back!"[25] In my analogy, the house of Judah represents one portion of humanity while the house of Israel represents another. The former represents those who have/will come to trust in Jesus in this life. The latter represents those who will not believe, even to the point of death.

The house of Judah viewed the house of Israel as though they were not physically related to Abraham. In their opinion, the house of Israel was not worthy of being called "Israel." As far as they were concerned, the "other" house was essentially gentile. Paul stated that "a partial hardening has come

21. Joseph was a type of the Christ before Moses came along.
22. That is, twelve minus one (Joseph).
23. Exod 3:7.
24. So had the entire world. Many see Israel as the people with the heritage, but the entire human race has a heritage in Adam.
25. Jim Staley explores this concept in his series entitled *Identity Crisis*. I do not necessarily support everything he claims in the video, although he makes several interesting points. It can be found on YouTube.

upon [the house of] Israel, until the fullness of the "gentiles" (the house of Judah) has come in. And in this way, all of Israel (both tribes) will be saved; as it is written: *The Deliverer will come from Zion, he will banish ungodliness from Jacob.*"[26]

"The Deliverer. . . will banish all ungodliness from Jacob.[27] If the house of Judah can represent those who are in Christ, we can say the ungodliness of the southern house has already been banished—all that remains is the ungodliness of the prodigal northern house (those who are not in Christ). In this way, all of Israel *will* be saved[28]—every knee shall *bow* and every tongue shall swear *allegiance*.[29]

A Cry for Justice

> The purpose of [Jesus'] sacrifice was not to change God's attitude toward us, but to change our attitude towards him.
>
> —THOMAS TALBOTT[30]

I am often asked why I am so passionate about the the doctrine of Universal Reconciliation. I am asked, "Don't the likes of Hitler and Stalin deserve ECT or annihilation, at least?" Do they? More than you or me. The Bible states that eternal life is to *know* God. Until we come to know God through Christ, we all experience a lack of life or the opposite of eternal life—aionian death—which does not disregard the necessity of postmortem judgment.

When this topic is actually discussed among fellow Christians, we rarely start the conversation by asking who deserves what. Instead, we question the justness of the doctrine in question. Some Christians believe ECT is just partially because they believe it coincides with the will of God, which seems to give the doctrine credence since God does no wrong.

Some take it a step further by claiming that God can justify any action simply by performing it. Yet that would suggest that his actions are unpredictable and arbitrary, that the objective laws of logic are relative to the subjective whim of God. On the other hand, it does not follow that God

---

26. Rom

27. Or Adam?

28. The existence of one analogy does not deny the truth claims of another. By putting this analogy on paper, I do not deny the truthfulness of other analogies that make totally different claims. They are completely separate entities.

29. Isa 45:23 (ESV).

30. Talbott, *The Inescapable Love of God*, 135.

does something because of its justness because that would imply that the standard for justice transcends the Transcendent. The only coherent option before us is this: "God's actions are just because justice is consistent with his nature. God cannot deny himself[31] by acting against that nature. God *is* justness."

One could not say that ECT, CI, and CU are equally plausible because only one is actually possible.[32] Only one of the three can possibly concur with his essence. For the longest time, Christians have warred over questions regarding whether or not we deserve this or that, whether or not justice is actually served if we experience this mode of postmortem judgment or that one. Yet the question that we all have apparently failed to ask is actually the most important and illuminating one: "What does Jesus deserve?"

Christians get so distracted about who deserves what for what they did or did not do, and lost in questions regarding the point at which one might lose an opportunity at grace and forgiveness, that they miss the entire message of the Gospel—that Jesus paid it *all*. Therefore, all to him *we* owe. Since Jesus died for all, all have died.[33] However, all will not be raised to life until justice is finally brought to victory. Justice is due for humanity's sin against Christ—their lack of faith in him.

As Paul participated in the ministry of reconciliation, he taught something that is rarely preached on today—the reconciliation of all things. There was a reason why God "overlooked the times of ignorance, but now commands all people *everywhere* to repent."[34] The immediate verse says it was "because he has fixed a day on which he will judge the world in righteousness by a Man whom he has appointed."[35]

Why has this day been fixed/scheduled? Why did he suddenly command everyone everywhere to repent? If we can discover the answer to those questions, we can better understand the broader concept. I believe God has "fixed a day on which he will judge the world" and suddenly commanded "everyone everywhere to repent" for the same reason that he can no longer "overlook sin."

It was not until Jesus was put to death, rose from the grave, and ascended to the right hand of the Father that God suddenly required universal repentance.[36] Jesus completed his role in the ministry of reconciliation. His

---

31. 2 Tim 2:13.
32. This is due to the law of non-contradiction.
33. 2 Cor 5:14.
34. Acts 17:30.
35. Acts 17:31a.
36. Why would God command universal repentance if he is not pursuing universal

followers have been given theirs. We were included in this ministry once Jesus accomplished his role because once Jesus proclaimed "it is finished," everyone's faith became Jesus' rightful possession. In other words, everyone *owes* Jesus their faith. Until he has it, Jesus suffers an injustice.

Once God made the Old Covenant obsolete[37] by providing assurance to all by raising Jesus from the dead,[38] he began to hold the world responsible for the only sin that cannot be forgiven in this age or in the one to come,[39] which is also the only sin that is responsible, according to the New Covenant, for the uncommitted's lack of a relationship with God—their rejection of Jesus as Savior and Lord.[40] If there is an "unforgivable sin," disbelief is it.

The uncommitted's rejection of Jesus as Lord does not invalidate his lordship. They will be held accountable for their disbelief because they are without excuse. Scripture states that "everyone who exalts himself will be humbled, and he who humbles himself will be exalted." God humbles us for our own good, but that is not the only reason for which mankind will be humbled. Salvation is just as much about Jesus getting what he deserves as it is about our own good. To bring down the proud is to humble them. Once God will have humbled the proud, they will be brought to their senses and, subsequently, subjected to Jesus.

Scripture states that every tongue will profess that Jesus is Lord *to the glory* of God the Father.[41] It also states that all who profess that *Jesus is Lord* will be saved.[42] Why does the church have such a difficult time putting two and two together? The Bible describes Jesus as a friend of sinners.[43] It also states that a friend loves at all times.[44] Could it be any clearer? Ray Stedman said it best: "Judgment is not God's way of saying, I'm through with you! It's not a mark of the abandonment of God. It's the last loving act of God to bring you back. It's the last resort of love."

---

reconciliation? As Scripture says, "His will cannot be thwarted."
37. Heb 8:13.
38. Acts 17:31b.
39. This implies that other sins can be forgiven in the age to come.
40. I am not suggesting that other sins are nonexistent.
41. Phil 2:11.
42. Rom 10:9.
43. Matt 11:19.
44. Prov 17:17.

12

Grace, Mercy, and Justice in Love: Holiness

> When God is our Holy Father, sovereignty, holiness, omniscience, and immutability do not terrify us; they leave us full of awe and gratitude. Sovereignty is only tyrannical if it is unbounded by goodness; holiness is only terrifying if it is untempered by grace; omniscience is only taunting if it is unaccompanied by mercy; and immutability is only torturous if there is no guarantee of goodwill.
>
> —RAVI ZACHARIAS
> ONLY IF...

IT MAY BE DIFFICULT to see at first, but, given the way those two sentences are put together, Zacharias seems to believe that the uncommitted have an *accurate* perception of God's attributes, even though it is entirely *different* than a believer's. He seems to believe that God's attributes are *actually* good for Christians, but tyrannical for the uncommitted; that God's attributes are rightly perceived as contemptuous by the uncommitted, since they are unbounded by goodness, untempered by grace, and so forth toward them. I beg to differ.

If the uncommitted are terrified by God's attributes, I would argue that they have a faulty perception of who God is. Although the uncommitted seemingly experience his attributes to their detriment, God's attributes are to the detriment of nothing, besides what is detrimental to what is his by right—our souls. His attributes are not and cannot be detrimental to anyone's soul because, if they were, that would mean that God denies himself by opposing what is his. If his attributes are detrimental to anything, it must be to our sinful condition because sin is detrimental to our souls.

Even though everybody's soul is obviously their own, our souls belong primarily to the Father because he fathered each and every one of them.

They also belong to the Son because he laid down his life for us all—we were "purchased at a price." Jesus does not purchase our souls upon conversion. Rather, he purchased them all at Calvary. The deed is done. All that remains is the delivery of his rightful possession. The method of delivery is up to us.

Many prefer to believe that they have *gained* God's favor by grace through faith when, in reality, everyone was chosen to *exist* by and in his good favor and to remain there forevermore. Jesus died for us because he favors us. If the uncommitted are not in his good favor *until* they commit their lives to Jesus, why is he called "the Savior of all people, especially of those who believe," instead of the "Savior of those who believe"?[1] He loved each of us before we were formed in our mother's womb and he will love us long after our bodies return to the dust.

The Bible teaches that love is *outwardly* focused rather than concerned primarily about its own glory.[2] Since God is Love, he is outwardly focused rather than concerned primarily about his own glory. Once all things are reconciled in heaven and on earth, creation will finally align with his will for it. Only then will he attain his rightful glory in and through *all* that he has made—through all that is his.

According to Psalm 145:9, "the Lord is good to all, and his mercy is over all that he has made." How much of *everything* has God made? If someone fails to repent before they die, are they no longer made by God? Are they no longer a part of "all"; toward and over which he is good and merciful? CI attempts to deal with this passage's implications by claiming that God is good and merciful to bring hell to an end through the annihilation of the wicked, but the process leading toward that end remains problematic.

The last portion of Romans 2:4 states that God's goodness is *meant* to lead us to repentance. That *is* its purpose. Will it fail in that endeavor for anyone? God is good to all, his mercy is over all, and his goodness is meant to lead us to repentance. Many respond as follows: "That is true. . . but we have free will!" We do, but that response does not resolve anything. Is our free will detrimental to God's goodness and mercy. Can the freedom of our will thwart his ultimate purpose? Not according to Job 42:2. "I know that you can do all things, and that no purpose of yours can be thwarted."

Holiness

Holiness can be intrinsic or it can be attained from an external source. Since God is intrinsically holy—the only of his kind—we cannot say that he was

---

1. 1 Tim 4:10.
2. The glory of God is the culmination and revelation of his expressive will.

"set apart" by some external agent. Since he *is* holy simply because of *who* he is, we should not be surprised if his character surpasses our expectations. Rather, we should expect the unexpected because he is good and holy.

Since God is good, we should ask "How is his grace, mercy, love, and justice good?". Do they determine what it means to be good or does goodness determine the meaning of those attributes? This is not an either/or dilemma. God is good, but he is also gracious, merciful, loving, and just. Therefore, those attributes are good and goodness has to do with grace, mercy, love, and justice.

Since his goodness correlates with grace and mercy, then it is good for grace and mercy to be new every morning—perpetual; since his goodness correlates with love, then it is good for love to be unfailing—relentless; since goodness correlates with justice, then it is good for his justice to be absolutely successful—victorious.

As I mentioned in Section 2, Calvinists and Arminians have been struggling to account for the repercussions of their presuppositions since they were formed. One side emphasizes God's sovereignty through hyper-determinism, which minimizes *our* responsibility. The other side emphasizes God's love through anti-determinism, which minimizes *God's* responsibility. Christian Universalism bridges the gap by suggesting a form of determinism that does not eliminate the responsibility of either party.

Predestination

> Blessed be the God and Father of our Lord Jesus Christ, who has blessed us in Christ with every spiritual blessing in the heavenly places, even as he chose us in him before the foundation of the world, that we should be holy and blameless before him. In love he predestined us for adoption as sons through Jesus Christ, according to the purpose of his will, to the praise of his glorious grace, with which he has blessed us in the Beloved. In him we have redemption through his blood, the forgiveness of our trespasses, according to the riches of his grace, which he lavished upon us, in all wisdom and insight making known to us the mystery of his will, according to his purpose, which he set forth in Christ as a plan for the fullness of time, to unite all things in him, things in heaven and things on earth. In him we have obtained an inheritance, having been predestined according to the purpose of him who works all things according to the counsel of his will, so that we who were the first to hope in Christ might be to the praise of his glory. In him you also, when

> you heard the word of truth, the gospel of your salvation, and believed in him, were sealed with the promised Holy Spirit, who is the guarantee of our inheritance until we acquire possession of it, to the praise of his glory.
>
> —EPHESIANS 1:3-14

As is customary in Paul's epistles, he begins his letter to the church in Ephesus by giving thanks to God for the spiritual blessings that God generously pours out on those who are in Christ. Thereafter, he gets down to business. One of his first remarks to this gathering of believers affirms that they were chosen in Christ, before the foundation of the world, for the purpose of being holy and blameless before God.

Calvinists and Arminians read four words in this passage through a different set of lenses and have, consequently, come to a totally different conclusion regarding Election/Predestination. It does not read: "He chose us *to* be in him before the foundation of the world." Neither does it read: "He foreknew who would believe and chose us accordingly." If Paul would have chosen either of those phrases, or a slight alteration of either, little could be said against the Calvinist's or Arminian's point of view. Rather, it states that "we" were chosen *in him*. "We" clearly refers to the recipients of the epistle—a particular group of believers, but "in him" is not one-dimensional. Neither is "we" necessarily exclusive.

There is nothing in any of Paul's writings to suggest that those who are currently uncommitted are excluded from "election". Calvinists and Arminians assume that exclusion is implied in one way or another. Christians Universalist disagree. We believe that everyone is predestined from the foundation of the world to be holy and blameless before him—everyone is expected to be transformed into the person that God designed them to be... *for he has commanded everyone everywhere to repent.*

We believe that Jesus is *the* chosen one, that *he* is *the* predestined one. Outside of Christ, no one is "chosen" or "predestined." When anyone finds grace, mercy, love, and justice in Christ, they become chosen/predestined in *him*. Just as we are considered righteous in Christ because we are clothed in his righteousness, so, too, are we chosen/predestined in Christ. Indeed, the Father "has blessed us in the Beloved."

This passage includes the verses around which this section is written—those pertaining to *the mystery of his will*. As we have observed, the mystery of his will has been "set forth in Christ as a plan for the fullness of time, to unite all things in him, things in heaven and things on earth."[3] Since

---

3. I.e., heavenly things and earthly things.

Scripture has decreed that *all things* will be united "in him", is it too much to believe that everyone will be saved? Are we not saved by being in Christ?

Since I believe that everyone was created by a good God, I also believe he had a good purpose in mind for each of us before we were formed in our mothers' wombs. He knew that the human race would fall before he made us. Therefore, he decided beforehand to shut us all up to disobedience so that he could justly have mercy on us all.[4] Romans 8:6 states that "to be carnally minded is death." Yet Revelation 21:4 promises that there will be *no more death*. What does that suggest about the lifespan of carnal minds?[5]

When Jesus hung on the cross he bore the sins of the world, died, was buried, rose from the dead, and left the sin he became in the grave. He took on our sins and became what Christians refer to as "our old man." When he died, our "old man" died; but Jesus rose and became *the* new man, with which Christians identify.

Christian Universalists do not deny the existence of hell. We simply have a different understanding of it, just as Calvinists and Arminians have a different understanding of predestination. You *could* say that we believe in a literal hell with literal flames. Whether or not there are literal earthly flames in an extra-dimensional realm is anyone's guess.[6] Like many before us, we believe that the fires hell consist of flames of unrelenting grace and perpetual mercy; that they are victorious flames of love that cannot be quenched until justice is brought to victory. In a nutshell, we believe that the flames of hell are holy; for God, indeed, is holy; he is a consuming fire and hell is an unquenchable expression of the mystery that is his will.

---

4. Rom 11:32.

5. Annihilation is, theoretically, the ultimate form of death. Although the soul, technically, does not exist, it is considered dead. Some may claim that it is nonexistent and cannot be referred to even as an "it" after it dies. One would have to appeal to memory wipes in order to annihilate any trace of a soul, since a concept is existent even if it is only in the mind. Yet, that would require a significant alteration of a believer's personhood. Our memory of the uncommitted is a large part of what makes us "us." It fails via Occam's razor.

6. The flames of hell are just as literal as God is literally a consuming fire.

Epilogue

Urgency

> As God's partners, we beg you not to accept this marvelous gift of God's kindness and then ignore it. For God says, "At just the right time, I heard you. On the day of salvation, I helped you." Indeed, the "right time" is now. Today is the day of salvation.
>
> —2 CORINTHIANS 6:1-2

BY NOW, WE HAVE examined key words around which each doctrine of postmortem judgment revolve and have discovered that they do not necessarily entail what is taught by church authorities at large. Those who know God, through Christ, enjoy eternal/aionion life *here and now*. It is not just some future residence that we should make down payments on in this life, but a present-perfect relationship that *deserves* to be restored immediately. Likewise, those who are not in Christ experience aionion death/condemnation *here and now*. It is not just some future consequence that they should strive to avoid before it is eternally "too late," but a present-perfect condition that *deserves* to be restored immediately.

We who believe that Jesus will draw all people to himself are frequently told that we are allowing our feelings to cloud our judgment. Although that is a dismissive assertion, I cannot deny that our feelings are involved in the process. The problem with that accusation is that it implies that our accusers do not allow their feelings to effect their theological beliefs. We were not created as machines, but as individuals with emotions that should not be ignored. A large part of what makes us human is the interlacing of the heart and the mind.

Our souls were created with the ability to "feel" because God is a God of feelings. When someone says that Christian Universalists err because they allow their emotions to roam freely as they interpret Scripture, they might as well be saying that God allows his emotions to cloud his judgment as he pursues Universal Reconciliation. They might as well be saying that God errs because he allows his feelings to get in the way when he offers grace in place of brute justice.

If they are correct about the death of the uncommitted, that it guarantees that they will suffer forever or be annihilated, should that not motivate believers to spend every waking second pleading with passersby before it is eternally too late? The fact of the matter is that few actually live their lives as though they believe in ECT or CI.[1] One could say that their dry cheeks testify against them.[2]

On December 17, 2014, a woman was charged for the murder of her son. When she was questioned by the authorities, she explained that she killed her young child to ensure that he would go to heaven. She believed that since her son had not passed the supposed "age of accountability," then he was safe from ECT.[3] Although Christian apologists claim that such cases are extreme examples or anomalies, it can be argued that their actions were/are completely justified by their beliefs about hell. What is one heinous, yet merciful,[4] sin against a loved one compared to the potentiality of endless agony?

It has been stated in churches across the world that the odds of someone converting to the Christian faith before they die decreases as they age. If that is true, would it not be merciful to cut someone's life short in order to give them the greatest gift of all—eternal life? Granted, we cannot possibly know whether or not anyone in particular will die unrepentant and only God (the source of life) is qualified to take it,[5] but can we really blame anyone for caring more about their loved one's eternal good than their own? John Calvin had a similar point of view as he condoned putting heretics to death in order to spare the masses from potential theological deceit, which,

---

1. Apathy is a telltale sign of disbelief.

2. This is a paraphrase of J. D. Leavitt.

3. Michael Stone, "Mom kills son believing boy would be better off in heaven," *Progressive Secular Humanist* (blog), December 17, 2014, http://www.patheos.com/blogs/progressivesecularhumanist/2014/12/mom-kills-son-believing-boy-would-be-better-off-in-heaven/.

4. Some have attempted to justify infant mortality during times of war and terrorism by claiming that God allows the lives of children to be cut short because those children would certainly have aged beyond the age of accountability, only to die unsaved.

5. Thus disregarding the authority God has given the government, as he has appointed each officer.

according to orthodoxy, could potentially lead many to suffer endlessly in hell.[6]

In the book of Romans, Paul was evidently beside himself at the thought of native Israel failing to obtain their inheritance, which was promised to them under the Old Covenant. He realized that the New Covenant had arrived and that they were waiting in vain for an inheritance that was *now* only available in Christ. Israel failed to realize that Abraham's children are those who possess the *faith* of Abraham rather than his genetic code. Therefore, they failed to inherit what was "rightfully" theirs.

Paul stated that he was willing to sacrifice his inheritance only if it would grant native Israel her inheritance.[7] It is generally assumed that Paul was willing to suffer in hell *forever* if only native Israel would be saved.[8] Is it possible to interpret this passage sensibly apart from prevalent presuppositions? If so, we have to resist the urge to assume that Paul was referring to ECT or CI when he expressed his willingness to give up his inheritance for the sake of many.[9] What did he mean by this? What was he willing to relinquish? What was the gospel according to Paul?

Paul saw eternal life as a present-perfect relationship with God. When he observed the Israeli masses, he wept because they *could not* know God as long as they rejected his Son—the final prophet that God would ever send them.[10] He loved Israel so much that he was willing to sacrifice his relationship with God to ensure that prodigal Israel would return to a right-standing relationship with their brokenhearted Father.[11] He was not as concerned with what may happen to them when they die than he was concerned about the present condition of their souls.[12]

Paul was not volunteering to undergo ECT or annihilation on their behalf.[13] Neither was he volunteering to forfeit the grace that he had obtained *through* faith so that Israel could obtain it *apart* from faith. That would nul-

---

6. He considered "heresy" as bad as cold-blooded murder—as the murder of a soul.

7. Many of Israel's promises were conditional upon upholding their end of covenant, which was usually associated with the Law in one way or another. Their failure to uphold their end of the bargain resulted in the formation of the New Covenant, which God had planned from the beginning.

8. Notice that if Paul suffered ECT or was annihilated to save the rest of Israel, native Israel will not have been saved in full.

9. "Imitate me as imitate Christ." "Do as I do, as I do as he did."

10. Matt 21:37.

11. Was Jesus not willing to do the same?

12. He understood that death was a continuum of the present-perfect condition of the heart/soul.

13. Neither did Jesus.

lify the work of Christ, after all. He loved Israel so much that he felt undone as he observed their aimless wandering without a shepherd. They were going through the motions with their head rather than with their heart.

Just as any good parent would sacrifice their better good for the good of their children, so, too, was Paul willing to surrender his better good for Israel. Paul knew God. Therefore, he understood his character. He knew the God of all-grace.[14] He knew *Jehovah Rapha*—the God who heals. He also understood that healing comes through Christ alone. Perhaps he hoped momentarily that a temporary breach in his relationship with God might bring Israel to a right-standing relationship *in Christ*, knowing full well that his relationship could be restored thereafter. Just as an unnatural branch can be grafted into the vine and a natural branch can be cut off, so, too, can what has been cut off regain its former status.

As we carry out the ministry of reconciliation, "it makes all the difference in the world whether we view our neighbor as a potential convert or as someone whom God already loves."[15] Calvinists believe that God has a special love for the Elect while Arminians believes that God's love is all-inclusive, although it fails for most. CU maintains that God's love is all-inclusive without damaging his sovereign will.

The Church at large shuns Christian Universalists from the evangelical fold[16] because they not only believe that our presuppositions discourage us from witnessing to the lost, but they also believe that they discourage the lost from being sensitive to God's call for "everyone everywhere to repent." They see salvation as an escape from postmortem repercussions more than they see it as an escape from bondage in and of itself.

Many tend to believe that CU is not evangelical, which may be the result of one presupposition in particular—that an appeal to the self-centered nature of the flesh is necessary when we reason with the uncommitted. Many assume that the benefits of faith must clearly outweigh the cost associated with denying the flesh if we are to evangelize the dying world effectively. It saddens me that so many Christians have such a difficult time seeing any incentive whatsoever in the gospel message apart from a doctrine of fear.[17]

When the benefits associated with faith are presented clearly, they clearly outweigh the supposed benefits of remaining enslaved to the harsh

---

14. Ὁ δὲ θεὸς πάσης χάριτος (1 Pet 5:10).

15. Philip Yancey, *Vanishing Grace: What Ever Happened to the Good News?* (Grand Rapids, MI: Zondervan, 2014), 44.

16. Gregory MacDonald's book *The Evangelical Universalist* sufficiently addresses this mindset. ("Gregory MacDonald" is a pseudonym for Robin Parry.)

17. Knowing that perfect love casts out all fear, I long for the day when this doctrine will be cast out, along with the fear that it invokes.

taskmaster of this world. When the gospel message is explained in light of UR, I believe we will witness leagues of wandering souls being drawn[18] to the cross, just as a single flame draws creatures to itself in the dead of night. Once evangelicalism is detached from a doctrine of fear, one of the largest stumbling blocks will be removed from the path of the uncommitted?[19] Granted, many may remain uncommitted even then, but it would then be due to their misconception of God or the hardness of their hearts rather than due to a defamation of his character. Don't just take my word for it. Consider Charles Slagle's testimony as he describes his presentation of UR to a group of hardened criminals:

> The Salvation of 125 Inmates
> January 2, 2003
>
> At last, here is that testimony about my preaching universalism in prison and the response that followed.
> First off I have to say, "WOE is me, if I proclaim not these glad tidings!"
> I'd go freaking bonkers if I couldn't. Can anyone relate?
> A few years ago I preached this whole gospel of universal reconciliation to 500 inmates in a prison close to Weatherford Texas. I'm talking about the "restitution of all things" that Peter preached to the temple authorities when he proclaimed the good news, recorded in Acts chapter three.
> The message? The same as usual:
>
> GOD WILL NEVER GIVE UP ON YOU—NOT EVER! SO YOU MAY AS WELL GIVE UP DOING YOUR OWN THING AND ENJOY HIS FRIENDSHIP, BECAUSE YOU ARE GOING TO SOONER OR LATER.
>
> Oh yes, I talked about "hell" and consequences. I talked, as Peter did of "utter destruction" from ignoring the One who is the Lamb slain from the foundation of the earth, the One Who loves them with His very life. I told them that we can all have as much hell as we want—perhaps more than we've bargained for as long as we run from Him. However, I also told them that if they opted to sin with such dedication that they spent the entire "ages of the ages" in the lake of fire before God got them straightened out, that He loved them TOO MUCH to lose them. I told them that

---

18. Or dragged.
19. Fear will drain the life out of any good thing.

His name is "UN-failing Holy Love" and He intends to live up to His name! I told them that this is the nature of the stubborn love of the "Hound of Heaven." I spoke also of the Good Shepherd who will not fail or be discouraged until He finds the very last lost sheep and establishes salvation throughout all the earth.

It was a fantastic experience. I spoke of Sodom's restoration prophesied in Ezekiel chapter 16.

I don't know how it happened, but I soon found myself "on a roll," spoofing the "eternal torment" lie and religiosity—while these guys stared at me like a tree full of owls for the first few minutes. I told them that the religious gospel "You can count on God IF He can count on you!" is NOT good news. I said, "Dudes, that stuff will put you in the hospital! Ever been to 'group'?"

Then I held out my hand as if to shake hands with some of them and said, "Hi! My name is Charlie, and I'm an alcoholic!" And it struck a familiar cord I guess. For suddenly they were roaring with laughter and shouting and whistling and applauding and hooting and saying, "AMEN!! You preach it, Charlie!!"

This kind of response continued from that moment until the end of my message. Wow... was it an experience...

I told the guys that God is NOT calling out a church to go to "pie in the sky in the sweet by and by." No! He's calling out CO-REGENTS and CO-DELIVERERS to inherit the nations with Christ. To s-p-r-e-a-d heaven throughout all creation until Unfailing Love Himself becomes "all in all."

Hehe. While all of this delightful uproar was going on, there were a few scribes and Pharisees present (some visiting church folk) who crossed their arms and scowled furiously while I was preaching. They were literally glaring daggers at me.

But I didn't care. I was having fun, and so were the guys. Besides, these religious scowlers brightened up considerably when "altar call" time came.

I concluded my message by saying, "Are you guys sick of religious crap? Do you want to LITERALLY AND PERSONALLY KNOW the Real Jesus who loves you with total and unconditional commitment? Do you want to be one of those deliverers He is now raising up to set creation free? Are you sick and tired of being a part of the problem and ready to be part of the Solution—Jesus Christ Himself?"

And the response?

125 of those tough looking dudes got up out of their chairs and came forward crying like little kids to receive Jesus Christ as their Lord and Savior. I then invited the Christians already

present (along with the scowlers who were now beaming and all teary-eyed themselves) to come pray with any of those men who had come forward to receive Christ.

Yep, those hard-core traditionalist Christians SURE LIKED THE RESULTS of the message, whaddayathink?

Closing out—

I find myself constantly praying that the Lord will protect those men (and others since that day whom the Lord has led me to touch) from religious folks who might come to "spy out their liberty in Christ." There are many who would seek to contaminate these newly born-again guys with churchianity's eternal punishment "winners and losers" toxin of conditional love. Many would like to convince them to believe that THEY sure were lucky they found the Lord before it was "eternally too late."

These men are in process of HEALING from the lie of conditional love—the lie that got them shut up in prison in the first place. Know what I'm saying folks?

They don't need this religious garbage.

These men were not saved by luck—nor were they saved by their wisdom. It was not their cleverness, nor was it mine, and neither was it "luck" that drew these hurting prisoners to Christ; it was the unfailing love and grace of God Himself!

So thanks for joining your prayers with mine for these guys (and other new Christians like them) as the Holy Spirit brings them to mind.

Love to all,

Charles Slagle[20]

Unashamed of the Gospel

In Paul's epistle to Rome, he stated that he was *not* ashamed of the gospel.[21] Many will ask, "Why would he be? What is there to be ashamed of?" Perhaps we should ask, "Why was he compelled to *deny* that he was ashamed of it?" If anything deserves our shame, it is ones unwavering commitment to a doctrine that scrambles the attributes of God and runs skeptics away from Christ. Section 2 examined four of these attributes in light of ECT, but there is one concept that I have saved for this moment to tie everything together.

20. Charles Slagle, "The Salvation of 125 Inmates [sic] Testimony," http://sigler.org/slagle/125_inmates.htm.

21. Rom 1:16a

Christians are so familiar with one verse in particular that many have managed to turn it into a cliché. Scripture teaches that those who trust in God "should not worry about tomorrow" because we are designed to live each day as though it is our last. Although we do have much to look forward to in light of eternity, we are given a special gift each day that we should cherish—*today*.

If ECT is true, it would be absurd for God to say that we should not worry for our unbelieving loved ones' tomorrow. What if they died tonight and woke up in the inescapable chambers of hell? To top it all off, we are also told to love our enemies—to care about *their* wellbeing. Many have turned this around by saying, "It is for this very reason that we should pray without ceasing." Pray for what? Their salvation? Why would we pray for their immediate salvation if we were not worried about their souls, about tomorrow?[22] In light of ECT, how can God expect us to love our neighbors, or even our enemies—to laugh with those who laugh and to cry with those who cry—without worrying about tomorrow?

Since Christian Universalists are not plagued with the anxiety that accompanies this doctrine, many doubt that we are able to evangelize the lost with any sense of urgency—that is, if we evangelize at all. However, as stated, perfect love casts out *all* fear. Since God *is* perfect love, *he* casts out all fear. He does not desire the kind of fear that tyrants indubitably crave. Since he knows the end from the beginning, he confidently tells us to refrain from worry. "The end" is *not* worthy of fear because it has been determined by he who loves us all with an unquenchable love—a kind of love that cannot fail.

As Christians, our primary objective in life is to love. Every commandment is fulfilled in this one commandment, after all.[23] Even so, it is within our nature to allow our egos to guide our choices, even if they are sincere and good-willed. What if the first decision we made each day was to love like Jesus loved, regardless of the consequences? Since Jesus is already in us, we should *strive* to allow him to be seen in us. We should allow Love to guide us and to drive *our* ministry. What if we stopped worrying about that which has never worried God and simply loved like him? What if we saw each day as a gift—as a day to love and be loved. Since he empowers us through the Holy Spirit to do just that, it may be much easier than we think.

"In my lifelong study of the Bible," says Phillip Yancey, "I have looked for an overarching theme, a summary statement of what the whole sprawling

---

22. If ECT is true, we should avoid forming and nurturing new friendships for our own peace of mind.

23. Gal 5:14.

book is about. I have settled on this: 'God gets his family back.'"[24] There is *no* greater hope or peace than that which can be found when one comes to realize that God loves our loved ones far more than we can imagine, that he cares about the greater good of each and every one of us, and that, in the fullness of times, he will unite all things in Christ.

When Jesus said, "the truth *will* set you free," he meant it. Jesus is the truth that will set you free, regardless of *who* you may be. The Hound of heaven loves *you* far too much to lose you. The same goes for those whom you love.[25] He loves them too. His love will not fail for them or for you, because it *cannot* fail. Neither can justice lose sight of victory.

As God's partners, we beg you not to accept this marvelous gift of God's kindness and then ignore it. At just the right time, God heard us. On the day of salvation, He helped us. *Today* is the day of salvation. Indeed, the "right time" is *now*.

---

24. Yancey, *Vanishing Grace*, 51.
25. He cannot love us fully without fully loving those whom we love.

Appendix A

Questioning the Gospel

CHRISTIANS DO A LOT of back slapping when it comes to belief in the gospel. It's like we're afraid to ask hard questions, struggle through difficult times, and doubt the faith. Jenny is a new Christian. She's well educated, thoughtful, terribly excited about the gospel, and acquainted with suffering. As we talked about her newfound faith, she explained to me that she tried church in the past. She'd had a "bad experience." I braced myself for some church trashing, but quickly realized Jenny had something to say to the church.

Jenny recounted story after story of her difficult questions being turned away by Christians and pastors. She was told, "All the answers are in the Bible. Just read it and have faith." Her doubts were dismissed as undermining skepticism. Eventually, despite her admiration for the church, she left. Why? She wasn't allowed to question the gospel.

The Bible Invites Doubt

Non-Christians aren't the only ones that need to question the gospel. On the other side of faith, our discipleship should be suffused with doubt. Many of us run from it. We look down on doubt. In contrast, the whole Bible presupposes doubt. The Bible is largely written by believers to believers who doubt their beliefs. Many saints were adept at questioning God, asking questions like:

- "Will you put to death the righteous with the wicked?" (Gen 18:25)
- "Oh, Lord, will you please send someone else?" (Exod 4:13)
- "Why do the wicked prosper?" (Ps 73)
- "How long Oh Lord?" (Ps 79)
- "Have you not rejected us, O God?" (Ps 60)
- "How will this be since I am a virgin?" (Luke 1:34)

- "My God, my God, why have you forsaken me?" (Matt 27:46)
- "Why do I do what I do not want?" (Rom 7:20)

These men and women questioned God, to his face. Thomas was incredulous when told about the resurrection. Facing Jesus, he still doubted. Just prior to the ascension, with the risen Jesus standing in their midst, we're told disciples ". . . worshiped but some doubted" (Matt. 28:17).

Recovering the Practice of Doubt

Christians have lost the practice of doubt. Instead, we often reinforce blind faith. We gather like-minded people around us to reinforce our beliefs, while isolating ourselves from genuine questions about God, Scripture, and life. Non-Christians see this and are put off. Some assume that Christianity is pure indoctrination. Others believe that you have to check your brain at the door of church. So they remain, on the outside of the church, with important, authentic questions about the gospel, with no one to hear them out.

We need to learn from our skeptical friends and neighbors. We need to be more honest about how bizarre our faith sounds. Have you ever considered that Christianity sounds like a cult? We purport that our leader died and rose from the dead, but that he is now, conveniently, invisible. We believe that he will reappear one day to set all things right. Do you really believe this? Why? Can you account for it in a believable way? Many of the gospel teachings are slipped onto the shelf of our mental library, where they gather to collect dust. Sure we "believe" them, but don't pull them down often enough to doubt them.

God has created a world filled with irony and incongruity. We are redeemed but we aren't. We are perfect in God's sight but not in real time. Jesus has defeated death and evil, but people die and suffer every day. Then, there's the everyday struggle to believe. We possess the promises of God, but fail to believe them every single day. Instead, we believe in the fleeting promises of the world. We believe the approval of co-workers is better than the enduring approval of God the Father. We believe holding a grudge will bring more satisfaction than giving away Christ's forgiveness. Suffering through a trial, we believe God is unjust or we are awful, instead of seeing God's grace and goodness to purify misplaced faith in ourselves or in the comforts of this world. O, how we disbelieve.

Blind Faith is blinding to the World

We disbelieve the gospel because we fail to doubt the gospel. We don't interrogate it to find better promises. We don't question God, asking him for greater joy than the fleeting satisfaction we have in comfort. We don't query the gospel to make better sense of suffering. Instead, we place one hand over our eyes, and point upward: "Just have faith." This is unbelievable. It is shallow.

Blind faith is blinding faith. It masks the light of the gospel, covering up the perceptive truths of Scripture that must be queried to be uncovered. People like Jenny need Christians who welcome, not stomp, doubt. An unbelieving world needs to see why the gospel is worth believing. They need to see what atonement has to do with pluralism, what regeneration has to do with environmental stewardship, what propitiation has to do with humility, what adoption has to do with sex trafficking, what justification has to do with self-esteem, what new creation has to do with the Arts, what union with Christ has to do with longings for significance. Our colleagues, coworkers, and neighbors also need to hear us doubt the gospel in face of: literature, homosexuality, racism, women, technology, pluralism, hypocrisy, evolution, and atheism, to name a few. The gospel must be questioned if we are to uncover its riches, not only for ourselves but also for the world.

Blind faith reroutes a detour around God's design in suffering. Peter reminds us that trials are meant to make us question, reflect, and refine our faith. When we suffer the loss of a friend, job, or dream, we are meant to question the gospel. We are meant to discover, through trial, how Christ is better, not just affirm that he is better. Suffering can show us how God is sufficient and the Savior is sublime. But we must doubt. We must take our hands off our eyes to stare our troubles in the face. Only then can faith become precious and perceptive. We've failed to realize we are meant to doubt our way into faith every single day. When we doubt the gospel, in God's presence, we find Jesus standing up in our circumstances, flooding them with hope.

Doubting for Joy

Standing in front of the risen Christ, "they worshipped but some doubted" (Matt 28:17). The disciples are skeptical. They possess the facts, the proofs to believe, but still don't have faith. Or maybe they believed but lacked faith? Making a distinction between belief and faith Harvard Religion scholar, Harvey Cox writes: "We can believe something to be true without it making much difference to us, but we place our faith only in something that is vital for the way we live." If we don't see the gospel as vital, then we will restrict it to the realm of belief. In other words, we can believe the gospel with it making very little difference to our lives. We can believe without faith.

The way forward from belief to faith is through the path of doubt, down the road of inquiry. We must question what we believe in order to increase in faith. For Christ to become vital, we must see how essential he is, in everything. We need the vital organ of faith. Belief cannot live without faith, the animating power of actual trust in a trustworthy gospel. This comes through testing our faith, asking how God is good in our pain, what Jesus has to do with Science, how the Holy Spirit changes on culture. We need to get in front of the face of God and ask the hard questions with humility. We need to pull the gospel off the shelf and doubt it for joy.

Seeing the resurrected Jesus, some disciples "disbelieved for joy" (Luke 24:41). Doubt arose in their hearts. Jesus patiently revealed his hands and feet, scarred from his crucifixion. This was no spirit. Touching his body, they tested their beliefs (that the resurrection wasn't plausible), and considered the immense promise this belief held if it were true. They leaned forward into faith. The closer they got to the risen Lord, under scrutiny, the more belief gave way to faith. They even watched Jesus perform an experiment, eating to prove he wasn't an apparition. The prospect of the gospel became more compelling as they questioned the gospel in the face of Christ. They disbelieved for joy. Like the wonder we feel when we hit a home run, ace the test, or win someone's affection, they disbelieved for joy. Stunned in awe, they couldn't believe it, but they were jumping up and down for joy inside. Disbelieving for joy, they fell headlong into faith.

Appendix B

Proof-texts

> It was on this account that the ancients invented those infernal punishments of the dead, to keep the wicked under some awe in this life, who without them would have no dread of death itself.
>
> —CICERO

DOES THE BIBLE UNDERGIRD the "orthodox" doctrine of hell? Apparently, many believe so. Otherwise, the masses would not wholeheartedly defend it. Many have claimed that the Bible says much more about hell than it does about heaven.[1] Although I disagree with that notion, no Christian would believe such a thing if the Bible did not *seem* to support it. However, anyone with a moderate amount of life experience should be well aware of the fact that things are not always as they appear.

Consider the following list of supposed proof-texts that have been used in support of the doctrine of ECT. Following each proof-text, I will make a brief statement regarding why each verse does not necessarily support prevalent presuppositions. What follows is something for the reader to think about. Let it resonate. I am not trying to stir debate—not just yet, anyway.

---

1. "Hell" is used in twenty-three verses in the King James Version of the New Testament. Out of its twenty-three usages, twelve of them are translated from "Gehenna." Of those twelve, nine of them are repeats of the same accounts in Matthew, Mark, and Luke, making only three usages. John never uses the term. Thus a small amount of research will discredit the erroneous assertion that the Bible speaks more about hell than about heaven. Jesus never threatened anyone with ECT. Only a small percentage of said usages are actually about postmortem judgment.

APPENDIX B

Forty Supposed Proof-texts for ECT[2]

1. Everlasting Punishment (Matthew 25:46)

Did you know the Greek word translated "eternal" in this verse and many others literally translates as "age-during"? Αἰώνιος/*aiōnios* pertains to "an age"/"the ages," according to every literal translation of the Bible.

2. Unquenchable Fire (Mark 9:43, 44)

Does "unquenchable" *certainly* mean "inextinguishable"?[3] The fire apparently does not obliterate the worm that "does not die." This does not imply that the human soul must suffer endlessly. The most it could imply is that the soul will not break down or cease to exist due to the flame. How would the original audience understand fire/sulfur?

3. The Second Death (Revelation 20:12–14)

Notice that "the second death" was identified as death and hell[4] being cast into the lake of fire. Those whose names were not in the book of life were mentioned after the identification of the second death rather than before. What could this suggest? Must the second death equate endless conscious torments?

---

2. D. P. Livermore, *Proof Texts of Endless Punishment, Examined and Explained* (Chicago: Emerson, 1862). http://www.tentmaker.org/books/proof_texts_on_endless_punishment.html.

3. Dr. Purcell stated, "It is crystal clear from The Holy Bible the word 'unquenchable' does not mean such a fire will never go out; it only means that it will not be extinguished or put out. All fires go out after the combustible material has been consumed. So, spiritually speaking, what is the combustible material fueling the fire of hell? It cannot be the bodies, since they are not consumed. The answer is 'sin'. Once sin has been burned up, purifying sinners, the fire of hell will go out as all fires do." Jesus' mixed metaphor for purification, "salted with fire," is proof positive that hell is time-limited, not eternal. — Purcell, Spiritual Terrorism, p. 325.

4. That is, the grave.

4. Salvation and Damnation (John 5:28–29)

Does a "resurrection to damnation" imply endless misery? Could this be one of the vague passages that needs to be interpreted in light of clearer passages rather than the other way around?

5. Ye Shall All Likewise Perish (Luke 13:3)

The Greek term for "damnation" in this verse is κρίσις/*krisis*, which is literally rendered as "judgment." If "damnation" simply means "judgment," why should we assume it implies endlessness? What does this reveal about proof-text four above?

6. The Damnation of Unbelief (Mark 16:16)

Must "damnation," which is literally rendered as "condemnation" or "judgment," be an endless punishment? Does the passage say anything about duration? Did you know that other versions of the Bible use "condemned" rather than "damned"? Is condemnation necessarily endless in its general usage?

7. Everlasting Contempt (Daniel 12:2)

The Hebrew word that is usually translated as "everlasting" is עוֹלָם/*'ôlām*. Its Greek equivalent is αἰώνιος/*aiōnios*. *'Ôlām* and *aiōnios* are figuratively translated as "the vanishing point," which paints a picture of something that is set at a distance that is too far off to be seen. Nevertheless, it is set at a *fixed* point in the distance. Many believe the term was originally understood in a practical manner. How does this relate to the "eternal" covenant regarding circumcision mentioned in Genesis 17:13? The New Testament teaches that circumcision is no longer required. How should that affect our interpretation of its usage elsewhere?

8. The Straight Gate (Matthew 7:13, 14)

Does "few"/"many" traveling through the narrow and broad gates necessarily mean that the destruction at which the many eventually arrive, and in some sense experience throughout the entire journey, is an endless one? Can destruction be endless without losing that which makes it destruction?[5]

9. The Case of Judas (Matthew 26:24)

If someone says it is better for them to never have been born, are they necessarily implying anything about postmortem judgment? Could this be hyperbole? Could it parallel Job cursing the day of his birth?

10. Sin unto Death (1 John 5:16–17)

Must this imply anything about the duration of a postmortem judgment? Could it simply refer to physical death? Humanity is spiritually dead before they are made alive in Jesus. If it refers to a sin unto the second death, can God not raise someone from the second death as efficiently as he can raise them from the first?

11. Hell for the Wicked (Psalm 9:17)

Does the wicked "returning to Sheol" say anything about the duration of postmortem suffering? Could that phrase be a colorful way of saying the wicked shall be put to death and return to the dust from which humans are formed?

12. Out of the Kingdom (1 Corinthians 6:9)

Does the mentioning of the fact that the unrighteous/unrepentant do not inherit the kingdom of God necessarily mean the wicked could never be transformed into that which inherits it? At one point or another, everyone was a child of wrath and unqualified to inherit the kingdom.[6] The unrighteous cannot inherit the kingdom as long as they are outside of Jesus and therefore unrighteous.

---

5. I will write more on this later.
6. Eph 2:3.

13. The Few Saved (Luke 13:23)

On which scale is this measured? Could it be saying that few will be saved from *experiencing* judgment, regardless of how long it lasts? Must it imply anything about whether or not the many, who will not avoid this judgment, will eventually be saved and restored with the rest of creation?[7]

14. The Rich Man and Lazarus—The Great Chasm (Luke 16:26)

Must the chasm imply anything beyond one's own inability to get up and leave either place or travel between them as they please? Does Christ not bridge each of our "chasms" by doing that which is impossible for humans? Some believe Lazarus represents gentiles and the rich man represents Jews.[8]

15. Hope of the Godless (Job 8:13)

Why must the phrase, "the hope of the lost shall perish," regard anything beyond this life, given that the surrounding verses mention how earthly possessions pass away? It does not explicitly say anything about the afterlife. Surely, the lost have no hope without the Holy Spirit securing their lives in Christ.

16. Sin against the Holy Spirit (Matthew 12:31, 32)

Is it *a matter of fact* that something which cannot be forgiven in this world/age can likewise not be forgiven in the next world/age, even if someone is repentant? Can this sin be understood as something that cannot be forgiven *as long as* someone is committing that sin? Can we determine a single sin that corresponds with this description? How about a rejection of the Holy Spirit's drawing of us to Jesus?[9] If we place our eschatological presuppositions aside, would this passage require an interpretation that corresponds with prevalent presuppositions?

---

7. Acts 3:21.

8. To use a modern analogy, if the Bible would have said that, after The Final Judgment, all those infected with sin will be cast into a fiery lake of penicillin, would that not logically symbolize healing sin infection? Sulfur was the wonder drug in the ancient world as penicillin is today. —Purcell, Boyd. Christianity Without Insanity. Charleston, SC: CreateSpace, 2012.

9. The notion of irresistible grace will be addressed elsewhere.

17. Fearful Judgments of God (Hebrews 10:31)

If the doctrine of ECT is not true, would "falling into the hands of the living God" not be worthy of fear? According to ECT, one moment of postmortem judgment is unbearable. Regarding the Greek term *apollumi* ("to destroy") in *An Expository Dictionary of Biblical Words*, W. E. Vine states, "The idea is not extinction but ruin, loss, not of being, but of well-being."[10]

18. In Danger of Hell Fire (Matthew 5:21–22)

Does being in danger of the hell[11] of fire say anything about the duration of judgment? For the Jewish culture, especially around the time of Christ, fire and brimstone had certain allegorical implications.[12]

19. Scarcely Saved (1 Peter 4:17, 18)

Is it possible that "the righteous" in this passage is referring to the self-righteous (Pharisees)? If so, "the righteous scarcely being saved" would then be emphasizing how legalism does not save. Could it not also be referring to earthly judgment, seeing how Christians and unbelievers experience judgment on earth for their sins?

20. Let Him Be Accursed (Galatians 1:8)

Does being accursed imply anything about its duration? The Greek term translated into "accursed" is derived from the Greek term ἀνάθεμα/*anathema*, which literally means "that which is laid up—a votive offering." It speaks of the thing offered to God which is literally cursed *to* death (for example, the sheep, goat, or bird on the altar, which foreshadows its antitype—the Lamb of God).[13]

---

10. Although this term does not appear in this verse, it is often applied to the concept of "falling into the hands of the living God."
11. That is, Gehenna.
12. Some translations use "liable to" or "guilty of" in place if "danger of".
13. Gal 3:13.

21. Everlasting Destruction (2 Thessalonians 1:6–9)

In the Greek language, "eternal destruction" comes from the term αἰώνιον ὄλεθρον/*aiōnion olethron* which is rendered as "age-during destruction." As mentioned in response to proof-text eight, can destruction be endless without losing that which makes it destruction?[14]

22. Laugh at Your Calamity (Proverbs 1:24–26)

Does this passage necessarily make any implications regarding postmortem judgment? The primary meaning of calamities pertains to natural disasters. The chapter concludes by suggesting that those who seek God will not have a fear of calamities/disasters *in life*. It also says many will diligently seek him, but will not find him. The Bible also teaches that those who *diligently* seek God *will* find him. Therefore, the former passage implies that their seeking of him is inauthentic or not diligent. Those who genuinely seek God, with diligence, will find him.[15]

23. God a Consuming Fire (Hebrews 12:29)

How does the reference to God as a consuming fire support ECT? Did you know that "fire and brimstone" signified purification and cleansing to the minds of first-century Jews?

24. Soul and Body in Hell (Matthew 10:28)

Humanity should have reverence for he who has authority over body and soul, but does the mentioning of a destruction of any sort support ECT? If destruction can never reach its goal— a moment of completion—it would lose the details that give it meaning. God destroys to make way for restoration.[16]

---

14. Consider similar terminology in Philemon 15.
15. Jer 29:13.
16. Consider the usage of "body and soul" as it refers to that of a forest in Isa. 10:18.

25. The Wicked Driven Away (Proverbs 14:32)

Can the overthrown not seek forgiveness? Does the grace of God ever become unavailable? If so, how does he express his unfailing love for those to whom grace is unavailable?

26. Impossible to Renew Them (Hebrews 6:4–6)

Does this necessarily imply God could never bring some people to repentance? Those who accept the doctrine of eternal security interpret this passage as a hypothetical scenario. It supports their idea that one could never have been sincerely saved only to become apostate because "once saved always saved"; if not, they would be crucifying Christ all over again.[17]

27. Eternal Judgment (Hebrews 6:1–2)

Besides the Greek term *aiōnion* pertaining to an age/the ages, have you ever considered that the punishment can be understood as eternal apart from an endless duration? For example, the fire on the altar was described as an eternal fire. The same goes for the fire that destroyed Sodom and Gomorrah. Is either still burning today?

28. And we are not Saved (Jeremiah 8:20)

I do not understand why some Christians use this verse as a proof-text for ECT, but they do. Someone can read into the text that God chooses not to save some people and thereby affirm that God seemingly does not desire to save some. However, that would contradict the passage that states that God does not desire for any to perish, but for all to come to repentance.

29. God's Indignation (Psalm 7:11)

Does indignation necessarily specify anything about postmortem suffering or its duration?

---

17. Heb 6:6.

30. Furnace of Fire (Matthew 13:42)

Throwing the unrepentant into a fiery furnace is definitely vivid imagery. Could the mention of a furnace here have something to do with the one in Daniel? Could the Christophany in Daniel imply something contrary to ECT? Must weeping and gnashing of teeth imply anything more than sorrow, regret, or discomfort, which leads to repentance and reconciliation by design?[18]

31. Damnation to Himself (1 Corinthians 11:29)

Many translations have chosen "judgment" instead of "damnation" in this passage and others.

32. Burn as an Oven (Malachi 4:1)

Does this burning of stubble, where there is no termination, not seem like an utter destruction whose completion could make way for the restoration that many other passages envision for all of creation?[19]

33. Hidden to the Lost (2 Corinthians 4:3)

Did you read the following verse that says it is Satan who blinds the lost? Could this veiling be the result of their refusal to repent? Since God desires to save all, in that he desires for all to come to repentance, why would he create a counterproductive mode of postmortem judgment? Since Scripture implies that this "veiling" occurs to the self-righteous, why should we assume that it is permanent? Once the self-righteous are humbled, what is there to prevent the veil from being lifted (as happened for Nebuchadnezzar)?

34. Draw Back to Perdition (Hebrews 10:39)

Again, is it possible for a destruction to never come to completion? God's destructions make way for restoration, inching toward his decree to reconcile all things in Christ.[20]

---

18. Consider the usage of this terminology in Deut 4:20.
19. Refer to Mal 3:1–5.
20. Col 1:19, 20.

35. Son of Perdition (John 17:12)

Did you know that some translations use "destruction" instead of "perdition"? The Greek word literally means "utter destruction," which cannot imply endlessness. Destructions have an end in mind—completion. Ἀπώλεια/ *apōleia* literally means "destruction, ruin, or loss," which says nothing about its duration. Neither does it imply that the destroyed cannot be restored. God aims to restore all things, even Sodom, for whom it will be more bearable on the Day of Judgment than for many with whom Jesus spoke.[21]

36. Lose His Own Soul (Matthew 16:26)

Did you know that some translations use the word "forfeit" instead of "lose"? Figuratively, the soul was understood as one's quality of life. Therefore, use of this word may have no postmortem implications. Even if it does refer to something beyond this life, does this necessarily prevent anyone from finding grace upon genuine repentance whenever it may come?

37. Agree with Thine Adversary (Matthew 5:25, 26)

While most people focus on the hyperbole ("never"), many miss its modifier—"until." Scripture frequently uses "eternal" as hyperbole when describing an event that seemed like it would never end, even though it eventually did. The same goes for references to fire as "unquenchable."

38. Wrath of God (Colossians 3:6)

Must the wrath of God never be satisfied? Will the Lord be angry forever?[22] If his anger will not last forever, how can the fires of hell burn "eternally"?

39. Cast the Bad Away (Matthew 13:47–50)

Must those thrown away never be restored? Did God not promise to restore all things? Was Saul not cast away in order for Paul to rise from the ashes?

---

21. Acts 3:21; Ezek 16:53.
22. Isa 57:16.

40. Forever and Ever (Revelation 20:10)

Did you know that most versions of the Bible have mistranslated this verse's conjunction to fit the mistranslation of *aiōnas/aiōnion*? The phrase translated as "forever and ever" is *aiōnas tōn aiōniōn*. As mentioned above, *aiōn* literally refers to an age/the ages. The Greek conjunction *tōn* does not mean "of," but "and." Yet "forever of ever" does not make sense. The phrase literally translates as "age*s* [feminine/masculine] of age*s* [masculine]." If translated literally, the assumed endlessness of the scenario is not as evident as many presume.[23]

It is natural to read our presuppositions into the Bible because we interpret it in light of how we view the world. The forty passages above are only a fraction of what could seem to support anyone's presuppositions as they casually read the Bible. Each of those passages once seemed to incontestably support my belief in ECT. Now that I no longer accept the doctrine, it is easier to understand how they do not imply that which I once presumed. The presupposition that ECT is a requisite of the Christian faith prevents many from considering any message contrary to it, even if alternate interpretations may have a richer and more glorious message. My aim is to assist in lifting that veil.

---

23. See Young's Literal Translation.

Appendix C

THE EARLIEST SYSTEM OF Universalistic theology was by Clement of Alexandria, who was the head of the theological school in that city until 202 A.D. His successor in the school was the great Origen who was the most distinguished advocate of this doctrine in all time. His mind has something of the largeness of Plato combined with Christian piety, and his influence was felt for many centuries throughout the East and to some extent in the West. The next great philosophical theologian in the East was Gregory of Nyssa. Then came Theodore Mopsuestia, distinguished as the promulgator of the grammatico-historical exegesis, and of a Biblical scientific theology containing a portion of the theory of evolution applied to the history of mankind. His influence for some centuries was more extensive than that of Augustine. Johannes Cassianus should also be mentioned. He was the author of Semipelagianism. Under the instruction of these great teachers many other theologians believed in universal salvation; and indeed the whole Eastern Church until after 500 A.D. was inclined to it.

In the West, this doctrine had fewer adherents and was never accepted by the Church at large. In the first five or six centuries of Christianity there were six theological schools, of which four (Alexandria, Antioch, Caesarea, and Edessa or Nisibis) were Universalist, one (Ephesus) accepted conditional immortality; one (Carthage or Rome) taught endless punishment of the wicked. Other theological schools are mentioned as founded by Universalists, but their actual doctrine on this subject is unknown.[1]

---

1. George T. Knight, "Universalists," in *The New Schaff-Herzog Encyclopedia of Religious Knowledge*, ed. Samuel Macauley Jackson (Grand Rapids, MI: Baker, 1950), 12:96. http://www.ccel.org/ccel/schaff/encyc12.u.ii.html#u.ii-Page_96.

Appendix D

Book Recommendations

Aulén, Gustaf. *Christus Victor: An Historical Study of the Three Main Types of the Idea of Atonement*. Translated by A. G. Herbert. Eugene, OR: Wipf and Stock, 2003. First published in English 1931 by SPCK.

Beauchemin, Gerry. *Hope Beyond Hell: The Righteous Purpose of God's Judgment*. With D. Scott Reichard. Rev. ed. Olmito, TX: Malista, 2010

Beecher, Edward. *History of Opinions on the Scriptural Doctrine of Retribution*. Edessa, 2014. Kindle edition.

Bell, Rob. *Love Wins: A Book about Heaven, Hell, and the Fate of Every Person Who Ever Lived*. New York: HarperOne, 2011. Kindle edition with audio and visual.

Gregg, Steve. *All You Want to Know about Hell: Three Christian Views of God's Final Solution to the Problem of Sin*. Nashville, TN: Thomas Nelson, 2013.

Hanson, John Wesley. *Universalism: The Prevailing Doctrine of the Christian Church during Its First Five Hundred Years*. Edited and expanded by David Mackey. Boston, MA: Universalist, 2014. First published 1899 by Universalist.

Leavitt, J. D. *A Heavenly Faith: Heretically Orthodox*. 2013. Kindle edition.

Lewis, C. S. *A Grief Observed*. New York: Harper, 1996. First published 1961 by Faber and Faber.

MacDonald, George. *Unspoken Sermons: Series i, ii, and iii*. 2012. Kindle edition. First published 1867–89.

MacDonald, Gregory [Robin A. Parry]. *The Evangelical Universalist*. 2nd ed. Eugene, OR: Cascade, 2012.

Purcell, Boyd C. *Spiritual Terrorism: Spiritual Abuse from the Womb to the Tomb*. Bloomington, IN: AuthorHouse, 2008. Kindle edition.

Richards, E. Randolph, and Brandon J. O'Brien. *Misreading Scripture with Western Eyes: Removing Cultural Blinders to Better Understand the Bible*. Downers Grove, IL: IVP, 2012.

Rogers, Ivan. *Judas Iscariot: Revisited and Restored; Discovering Grace in an Unlikely Place*. Maitland, FL: Xulon, 2008.

Talbott, Thomas. *The Inescapable Love of God*. 2nd ed. Eugene, OR: Cascade, 2014.

Van der Merwe, Andre. *Grace, the Forbidden Gospel*. Bloomington, IN: WestBow, 2011.

Young, Wm. Paul. *The Shack*. In collaboration with Wayne Jacobsen and Brad Cummings. Newbury Park, CA: Windblown, 2007.

Appendix E

George MacDonald on Adoption

"Is God then not my Father," cries the heart of the child, "that I need to be adopted by him? Adoption! that can never satisfy me. Who is my father? Am I not his to begin with? Is God not my very own Father? Is he my Father only in a sort or fashion—by a legal contrivance? Truly, much love may lie in adoption, but if I accept it from any one, I allow myself the child of another! The adoption of God would indeed be a blessed thing if another than he had given me being! but if he gave me being, then it means no reception, but a repudiation.—'O Father, am I not your child?'"

"No; but he will adopt you. He will not acknowledge you his child, but he will call you his child, and be a father to you."

"Alas!" cries the child, "if he be not my father, he cannot become my father. A father is a father from the beginning. A primary relation cannot be superinduced. The consequence might be small where earthly fatherhood was concerned, but the very origin of my being—alas, if he be only a maker and not a father! Then am I only a machine, and not a child—not a man! It is false to say I was created in his image!

"It avails nothing to answer that we lost our birthright by the fall. I do not care to argue that I did not fall when Adam fell; for I have fallen many a time, and there is a shadow on my soul which I or another may call a curse; I cannot get rid of a something that always intrudes between my heart and the blue of every sky. But it avails nothing, either for my heart or their argument, to say I have fallen and been cast out: can any repudiation, even that of God, undo the facts of an existent origin? Nor is it merely that he made me: by whose power do I go on living? When he cast me out, as you say, did I then begin to draw my being from myself—or from the devil? In whom do I live and move and have my being? It cannot be that I am not the creature of God."

"But creation is not fatherhood."

"Creation in the image of God, is. And if I am not in the image of God, how can the word of God be of any meaning to me? 'He called them gods to whom the word of God came,' says the Master himself. To be fit to receive his word implies being of his kind. No matter how his image may have been defaced in me: the thing defaced is his image, remains his defaced image—an image yet that can hear his word. What makes me evil and miserable is, that the thing spoiled in me is the image of the Perfect. Nothing can be evil but in virtue of a good hypostasis. No, no! nothing can make it that I am not the child of God. If one say, 'Look at the animals: God made them: you do not call them the children of God!' I answer: 'But I am to blame; they are not to blame! I cling fast to my blame: it is the seal of my childhood.' I have nothing to argue from in the animals, for I do not understand them. Two things only I am sure of: that God is to them 'a faithful creator;' and that the sooner I put in force my claim to be a child of God, the better for them; for they too are fallen, though without blame."

"But you are evil: how can you be a child of the Good?"

"Just as many an evil son is the child of a good parent."

"But in him you call a good parent, there yet lay evil, and that accounts for the child being evil."

"I cannot explain. God let me be born through evil channels. But in whatever manner I may have become an unworthy child, I cannot thereby have ceased to be a child of God—his child in the way that a child must ever be the child of the man of whom he comes. Is it not proof—this complaint of my heart at the word Adoption? Is it not the spirit of the child, crying out, 'Abba, Father'?"

"Yes; but that is the spirit of adoption; the text says so."

"Away with your adoption! I could not even be adopted if I were not such as the adoption could reach—that is, of the nature of God. Much as he may love him, can a man adopt a dog? I must be of a nature for the word of God to come to—yea, so far, of the divine nature, of the image of God! Heartily do I grant that, had I been left to myself, had God dropped me, held no communication with me, I could never have thus cried, never have cared when they told me I was not a child of God. But he has never repudiated me, and does not now desire to adopt me. Pray, why should it grieve me to be told I am not a child of God, if I be not a child of God? If you say—Because you have learned to love him, I answer—Adoption would satisfy the love of one who was not but would be a child; for me, I cannot do without a father, nor can any adoption give me one."

"But what is the good of all you say, if the child is such that the father cannot take him to his heart?"

"Ah, indeed, I grant you, nothing!—so long as the child does not desire to be taken to the father's heart; but the moment he does, then it is everything to the child's heart that he should be indeed the child of him after whom his soul is thirsting. However bad I may be, I am the child of God, and therein lies my blame. Ah, I would not lose my blame! in my blame lies my hope. It is the pledge of what I am, and what I am not; the pledge of what I am meant to be, what I shall one day be, the child of God in spirit and in truth."

"Then you dare to say the apostle is wrong in what he so plainly teaches?"

"By no means; what I do say is, that our English presentation of his teaching is in this point very misleading. It is not for me to judge the learned and good men who have revised the translation of the New Testament—with so much gain to every one whose love of truth is greater than his loving prejudice for accustomed form;—I can only say, I wonder what may have been their reasons for retaining this word *adoption*. In the New Testament the word is used only by the apostle Paul. Liddell and Scott give the meaning—'Adoption as a son,' which is a mere submission to popular theology: they give no reference except to the New Testament. The relation of the word [Greek: *niothesia*] to the form [Greek: *thetos*], which means "taken," or rather, "*placed* as one's child," is, I presume, the sole ground for the so translating of it: usage plentiful and invariable could not justify that translation here, in the face of what St. Paul elsewhere shows he means by the word. The Greek word *might* be variously meant—though I can find no use of it earlier than St. Paul; the English can mean but one thing, and that is not what St. Paul means. 'The spirit of adoption' Luther translates 'the spirit of a child;' *adoption* he translates *kindschaft*, or *childship*."

Of two things I am sure—first, that by *niothesia* St. Paul did not intend *adoption*; and second, that if the Revisers had gone through what I have gone through because of the word, if they had felt it come between God and their hearts as I have felt it, they could not have allowed it to remain in their version.

Once more I say, the word used by St Paul does not imply that God adopts children that are not his own, but rather that a second time he fathers his own; that a second time they are born—this time from above; that he will make himself tenfold, yea, infinitely their father: he will have them back into the very bosom whence they issued, issued that they might learn they could live nowhere else; he will have them one with himself. It was for the sake of this that, in his Son, he died for them.

Let us look at the passage where he reveals his use of the word. It is in another of his epistles—that to the Galatians: iv. 1-7.

"But I say that so long as the heir is a child, he differeth nothing from a bondservant, though he is lord of all; but is under guardians and stewards until the term appointed of the father. So we also, when we were children, were held in bondage under the rudiments of the world: but when the fulness of the time came, God sent forth his Son, born of a woman, born under the law, that he might redeem them which were under the law, that we might receive the adoption of sons. And because ye are sons, God sent forth the Spirit of his Son into our hearts, crying, Abba, Father. So that thou art no longer a bondservant, but a son; and if a son, then an heir through God."

How could the Revisers choose this last reading, "an heir through God," and keep the word *adoption*? From the passage it is as plain as St. Paul could make it, that, by the word translated *adoption*, he means the raising of a father's own child from the condition of tutelage and subjection to others, a state which, he says, is no better than that of a slave, to the position and rights of a son. None but a child could become a son; the idea is—a spiritual coming of age; *only when the child is a man is he really and fully a son.* The thing holds in the earthly relation. How many children of good parents—good children in the main too—never know those parents, never feel towards them as children might, until, grown up, they have left the house—until, perhaps, they are parents themselves, or are parted from them by death! To be a child is not necessarily to be a son or daughter. The childship is the lower condition of the upward process towards the sonship, the soil out of which the true sonship shall grow, the former without which the latter were impossible. God can no more than an earthly parent be content to have only children: he must have sons and daughters—children of his soul, of his spirit, of his love—not merely in the sense that he loves them, or even that they love him, but in the sense that they love like him, love as he loves. For this he does not adopt them; he dies to give them himself, thereby to raise his own to his heart; he gives them a birth from above; they are born again out of himself and into himself—for he is the one and the all. His children are not his real, true sons and daughters until they think like him, feel with him, judge as he judges, are at home with him, and without fear before him because he and they mean the same thing, love the same things, seek the same ends. For this are we created; it is the one end of our being, and includes all other ends whatever. It can come only of unbelief and not faith, to make men believe that God has cast them off, repudiated them, said they are not, yea never were, his children—and he all the time spending himself to make us the children he designed, foreordained—children who would take him for their Father! He is our father all the time, for he is true; but until we respond with the truth of children, he cannot let all the father out to us; there is no place for the dove of his tenderness to alight. He is our father, but we are not his children. Because we are his children, we must become his sons and daughters. Nothing will satisfy him, or do for us, but that we be one with our father! What else could serve! How else should life ever be a good! Because we are the sons of God, we must become the sons of God.[1]

---

1. George MacDonald, "Abba, Father!" in *Unspoken Sermons: Series i, ii, and iii.* 2012. Kindle edition. First published 1867–89.

www.ingramcontent.com/pod-product-compliance
Lightning Source LLC
Chambersburg PA
CBHW072145160426
43197CB00012B/2256